GRAVITY AND GRACE

Studies in Christianity and Literature 2

GRAVITY AND GRACE

Seamus Heaney and the Force of Light

John F. Desmond

BAYLOR UNIVERSITY PRESS

Cover Design by by Dustin Steller, Five Loaves Creative
Book Composition by Scribe, Inc.

Gravity and Grace by Simone Weil, translated by Arthur Wills, copyright ©1952, renewal ©1980 by G. P. Putnam's Sons. Original French copyright ©1947 by Librairie Plon. Used by permission of G. P. Putnam's Sons, a division of Penguin Group (USA) Inc.

Reprinted by permission of Farrar, Straus and Giroux, LLC: Excerpts from "Limbo," "Station Island," "Westering," "Settings xxii," "Toome," "Sibyl," "The Errand," "The Rain Stick," "Weighing-In," "Mycenae Lookout," "St. Kevin and the Blackbird," "The Settle Bed," "Damson," "Two Lorries," "The Gravel Walks," "Poet's Chair," "Keeping Going," "The Swing," "A Sofa in the 40's," "Mint," "The Tollund Man," "Tollund," "A Dog Was Crying Tonight in Wicklow Also," "Lightenings I," "At Banagher," "Whitby-sur Moyola," "At the Wellhead," "Postscript" from *Opened Ground: Selected Poems 1966–1996* by Seamus Heaney. Copyright ©1998 by Seamus Heaney; Excerpts from "Settings xxi," "Seeing Things II (Claritas)," "Lightenings viii," "To a Dutch Potter in Ireland," "Demond" from *Seeing Things* by Seamus Heaney. Copyright ©1991 by Seamus Heaney; Excerpts from "The First Words," "The Poplar" from *The Spirit Level* by Seamus Heaney. Copyright ©1996 by Seamus Heaney; Excerpts from "On His Work in the English Tongue," "At Toomebridge," "Bodies and Souls I" from *Electric Light* by Seamus Heaney. Copyright ©2001 by Seamus Heaney.

Library of Congress Cataloging-in-Publication Data

Desmond, John F.
  Gravity and grace : Seamus Heaney and the force of light / John F. Desmond.
    p. cm.—(Studies in Christianity and literature ; 2)
  Includes bibliographical references and index.
  ISBN 978-1-60258-067-1 (acid-free paper)
  1. Heaney, Seamus, 1939—Criticism and interpretation. 2. Heaney, Seamus, 1939—Religion. 3. Heaney, Seamus, 1939—Philosophy. 4. Weil, Simone, 1909–1943—Influence. 5. Spirituality in literature. I. Title. II. Title: Seamus Heaney and the force of light.

  PR6058.E2Z64 2009
    821'.914—dc22   2008029513

To my wife, Linda, in gratitude for her steadfast support and encouragement

Two forces rule the universe: light and gravity.
Works of art help us through the mere fact that they *exist*.
If we had chlorophyll we should feed on light as trees do.
Christ is that light.

—Simone Weil
Gravity and Grace

CONTENTS

Acknowledgments

First and foremost, I want to thank the many students who have studied Seamus Heaney's poetry with me over the years. Their interest, wonder, and challenging questions have always been the counterpoint that helped me to articulate and refine my own thinking about the poems.

I wish to thank Carey Newman and Roger Lundin of the Baylor University Press for their support of this project and their unfailing kindness and patience. As well, I appreciate the work of Elisabeth Wolfe for her careful editing and goodwill in seeing the manuscript to publication.

I owe a special debt of gratitude to professor Anthony Low, who read an early version of the manuscript and offered strong encouragement and useful advice at a critical juncture in the project.

Most of all, I want to express my deepest appreciation to Seamus Heaney, not only for his brilliant poetry but also for his steady encouragement of my work and his personal generosity and warmth during his visit to Whitman College in February 1999.

INTRODUCTION

In his impressive study of Seamus Heaney's literary aesthetic, *Seamus Heaney: Searches for Answers* (2003), Eugene O'Brien argues that Heaney's "epistemology of poetry" is rooted in a postmodern, Derridean, pluralistic vision of language and culture, a vision that creates a dialectical "field of force" in which the poet, the subject, and the reader are transformed and enabled to transcend inherited patterns of thought and action (1–8). The goal of Heaney's prose and poetry, according to O'Brien, is to broaden the meaning of Irish identity by developing an "inclusive consciousness" that engages the "other" at every level—personal, cultural, linguistic, religious, political, social, and ethical—in order to transfigure what has been inherited and "further" the human impulse toward greater individual and communal self-realization. O'Brien states his argument succinctly:

> In both his poetry and his prose, Heaney participates in a transformative discourse which exfoliates the fixed ideological positions of Catholic-nationalist-republican and Protestant-loyalist-unionist by probing their borders, their points of limitation. By then locating them within these broader and more expansive contexts, Heaney's writing transforms points of closure into points of opening to the other. Working at the level of individual consciousness, Heaney gradually creates the plural, complex and fluid "state of mind" of an Ireland which is open to its future. (5–6)

As his statement reveals, O'Brien understands Heaney the poet to be a cultural revisionist, one who "participates in what might be called the deconstruction of a monological historical narrative, bringing out the strains, fractures, aporias and antinomies that have been attenuated by the narrative sweep" (2).

1

In this regard, O'Brien sees Heaney's writing project as closely akin to that of Jacques Derrida in its emphasis on alterity and difference, its rejection of any so-called essentialist view of language and culture, and its sociopolitical conception of ethical responsibility and of personal and communal transcendence.

What is interesting and in my view somewhat surprising about O'Brien's fine study of Heaney's epistemology of poetry is his exclusion of any discussion of a metaphysical dimension of meaning in Heaney's writing, that is, of an order of reality independent of human construction. Indeed, the possibility of such a dimension is largely dismissed by O'Brien as part of the religious essentialism Heaney inherited from Northern Irish Catholicism—viewed as a monolithic, static structure of belief—and out of which Heaney the pluralist has allegedly grown. O'Brien holds this view of Heaney as a pluralist despite the poet's statement in an interview with Karl Miller that he conceives of poetic inspiration as *numen* and as grace, which are central notions in the "Catholic vision of an expanding universe" he learned as a youth (Miller 2000, 32–33, 36). Throughout O'Brien's study, notions of transfiguration and transcendence are invoked but almost always in the context of sociopolitical realities viewed within a mundane framework of meaning. O'Brien views the locus of meaning in Heaney's work entirely within what I would call a horizontal historical perspective rather than in terms of any possible vertical, i.e., metaphysical or transcendent, perspective. O'Brien's approach leads him like Derrida to emphasize, correctly in my view, the ethical importance of Heaney's writings, his significance as a cultural commentator and potential shaper of a better future. Nevertheless, given the historicist perspective of O'Brien's (and Derrida's) views on language, identity, transcendence, and the relationship between poetry and culture, one must still ask: what is the fundamental *ground* for such notions in Heaney's work? To put the question more precisely: what are the real ontological and religious bases for Heaney's epistemology of poetry and his hope for the future, given the fluid cultural situation as well as his own development as a person and a poet? Is there any room for a spiritual dimension that transcends, yet is intimately involved in, the mundane realities presented in his poetry, as his comment about his belief in poetic inspiration as grace (*numen*) seems to suggest? Stated differently, is there a vertical axis of meaning implicit in his poetry, one that intersects and counterbalances his concern with mundane historical realities, i.e., with what I would call the horizontal thrust of his poems.

My own view is that Heaney's aesthetic is grounded in a firm ontology based upon belief in the reality of a transcendent metaphysical order that is the ultimate source of meaning in his work and of the goal of "inclusive consciousness" he has prescribed for poetry. Belief in this metaphysical order is the ontological axis of his poetry, the intersection or crossroads between what he has called the "glimpsed ideal" and the specific mundane realities recorded in his major poems, especially since *The Haw Lantern* (1987). Moreover, I believe this ontology informs his view of language, which for all its concern with the philological and cultural permutations of words, is nevertheless rooted in the tradition of philosophical realism rather than in the structuralist or poststructuralist theories that devolve from deconstruction, even though these recent linguistic developments have certainly influenced his writing. That is, Heaney's realism posits language to be dynamic and evolving but rooted in a transcendent order of being that enables us to define true realities. These realities can be elucidated and measured in terms of universal standards of value manifested in the concrete language of each poem. This realist ontology also informs Heaney's ethical perspective, I believe, so that his notions of inclusiveness and his embrace of what is called "alterity" are based on a metaphysical view of human nature and of community that transcends, yet informs, the particular historical realities represented in the poems.

Moreover, I will argue that Heaney's ontology his view of language, and his ethics are compatible with a Christian anthropological view of humanity, with the essential doctrines of the faith, and with the ideal Christian vision of community, all of which help to shape what he calls the "field of force" in his poems. But to see his ontology and his aesthetic in this way, it is necessary to recognize, as indeed O'Brien and several other critics do, that Heaney has long ago outgrown the rigidly monolithic cultural Catholicism he imbibed in childhood, while at the same time retaining, testing, and poetically transforming many of its essential beliefs. Heaney's scrutinizing of that fundamental Christian vision in his poetry is much more complicated and nuanced than any inherited cultural form of belief suggests, as we shall see. His view of cultural Catholicism is often ironic, especially in his early poems, but his view evolves into more subtle representations as his career progresses.

Heaney acknowledged in his interview with Karl Miller the importance of his early Catholic training, its religious vision, and its language for poetry:

> For a poet, the one invaluable thing about a Catholic upbringing is the sense of the universe you're given, the sense of a light-filled, Dantesque, shimmering order of being. You conceive of yourself at the beginning of a sort of dewdrop, in the big web of things, and I think this is the very stuff of lyric poetry. After my parents died, the words which my secular education had taught me to be afraid of, words like "soul" and "spirit," came back and I said, "Damn it, these words have to be used—they mean something." And

> I felt that this dimension of reality, which I had in a sense schooled myself
> out of, must be risked somehow. So there's a certain exhilaration and risk
> about re-entering the baby language of my faith. (36)

Heaney went on to speak more precisely about the importance of his Catholic
upbringing for poetry:

> I think poetry has as much to do with *numen* as with hegemony. I have some
> notion of poetry as a grace, and I'm coming to believe that there may have
> been something far more important in my mental formation than cultural
> nationalism or the British presence or any of that stuff: namely, my early
> religious education. From a very early age, my consciousness was always
> expanding in response to the expanding universe of Catholic teaching about
> eternity and the soul and the sacraments and the mystical body and the
> infinite attentiveness of the Creator to your inmost thoughts. I didn't have
> to wait to read the *Paradiso* to know the vision it enshrines. (32–33)

Heaney's statements to Miller reveal his sensitiveness to the dynamics of his
own mental growth, especially how from an early age his mind was respond-
ing to the essential beliefs of Catholic teaching despite its narrow cultural
manifestations in Northern Ireland. His belief in the link between his mental
development and Catholic teaching can be seen, I believe, as an important
basis for his notion of poetry as a way to both express "inclusive consciousness" and to "further" the human spirit. In addition, his belief in poetry as
a "grace" indicates that he sees some correlation between the conventional
notion of muse-inspired poetic creation and the Catholic doctrine of grace;
that is, grace as a supernatural gift and not merely some personal talent or
effort of the human will.

    Of course Heaney's claim for the link between his Catholic upbringing,
his developing consciousness, and his poetry raises the complicated question
of his relation to the Catholic tradition in general and to that tradition as
it has been shaped by the political and religious situation in Northern Ireland. As Michael Parker has shown, County Derry Catholicism in the years
1939–72 (Heaney moved to the Republic of Ireland in 1972) both nurtured
and stunted Heaney's developing identity. "It founded him, but at the same
time made him and his people founder" (1993, 115). The "blueprint for the
spirit" prescribed by the parochial church in those postwar years emphasized
toleration of evil and forgiveness of enemies. In so doing, it often became a
"straightjacket" in the face of the oppression leveled against the ever-enraged
Catholic minority. Violence became the routine response of many citizens,
both Catholic and Protestant. As a young adult, Heaney renounced sectarian
violence by both sides, but he identified emotionally with his own side—the

Catholic community. As an emerging author, he defined himself as a Catholic writer but emphasized "the cultural rather than the religious load implicit in that term" (Parker 1993, 115). Heaney spoke of his complicated predicament in an interview with Randy Brandes:

> As a member of the minority, solidarity was expected; and yet you were not just behaving in accordance with expectations, you were behaving naturally along ingrained emotional grain lines. But there is a second command besides the command to solidarity—and that is to individuate yourself, to become self-conscious, to liberate the consciousness from the collective pieties. (Qtd. in Parker 116)

As Parker points out, Heaney's drive for greater self-consciousness and individuation was fostered by his reading of Carl Gustav Jung, which helped liberate him from the "straightjacket" of cultural Catholicism into other modes of thought and feeling, especially by exploring pre-Christian and mythical sources of identity. Heaney's search for a more integrated self led him to "search for myths which would restore 'purpose and value' to life, which would incorporate Christian values and yet be free of 'conventional Christianity,' which would bring about a rapprochement 'between the conflicting sides of his own nature'" (116).

Parker's statement about Heaney's search for myths to restore "purpose and value" to life so as to "incorporate Christian values" free of conventional Christianity needs more precise analysis. The statement seems to accept the stereotype of "conventional Christianity" as somehow distinct from "Christian values." It offers this simple dichotomy without discussing any of the essential beliefs Heaney pointed to as formative of his consciousness—beliefs about eternity, the soul, the sacraments, the mystical body, and the Creator's "attentiveness" to individual consciousness. Because it ignores Heaney's own words, it fails to address the question of how these essential beliefs may actually have shaped his adult consciousness and poetry.

Heaney's actual situation as a young man growing out of narrow cultural Catholicism can be better understood, I believe, by seeing it through the intellectual perspectives offered by fellow poet Czeslaw Milosz and the French philosopher Simone Weil. Weil was an important influence on Milosz's thought and writing; Milosz, in turn, has exercised considerable influence on Heaney's thought and art, I believe. Throughout my study, Milosz will often serve as a bridge between Heaney and Weil.

Heaney's stance vis-à-vis Northern Irish cultural Catholicism and Christianity's essential doctrines needs to be examined within the broader context of the intellectual ground-shifts Milosz and Weil saw occurring in post–World

War I Europe. In his essay "Speaking of a Mammal," Milosz described the transformation of the age-old belief in man as a metaphysical being to the modern belief in man as a historical being, that is, as a creature defined totally by his subjection to the forces of history (2001, 214–19). In this transformation, propelled strongly by the rational scientific viewpoint, belief in the metaphysical dimension of human nature and of reality in general was rejected. What replaced it was a view of man as solely a creature of history, one who "is submitted to society to such an extent that the very air he breathes is conditioned by it" (215). Yet despite this transformation, Milosz argued that "man cannot be reduced to just a part of history" because he is a creature with soul and freedom of choice, fundamental qualities that transcend "history." Given the pressures exerted throughout advanced Western society in favor of the historicist view of man, Milosz surmised accurately that the essential question faced by moderns became an anthropological one: "What is man?" Corollary to this question, necessarily, is a second one: "What, for man, is value?" Viewing this crisis, Milosz pinpointed the importance of Simone Weil: "her attention is concentrated on the central problem of recovering the notion of human nature" (216).

Milosz and Weil—and to a great degree Heaney—understand man to be a metaphysical being, i.e., a person who possesses a spiritual soul, personal freedom, and an innate drive for transcendence yet who is also rooted in the historical world governed by what Weil termed the force of "gravity" or necessity. Hence, man's status is "contradictory," as Weil noted:

> The essential contradiction in human life is that man, having as his very being a striving toward the Good, at the same time is submitted in all his being, in his thought as well as in his body, to a blind necessity that is absolutely indifferent to the Good. This is the way things are; and this is why no human thinking can escape from the contradiction. (Milosz 2001, 216)

Stated differently, man's human condition as a contradictory being situates him in between the transcendent and the mundane, in what Weil called the *metaxu*.

At the same time, Milosz argued in his essay "Religion and Space" that under the pressure of historicism, modern man has "experienced the collapse of hierarchical space," that is, the belief that the order of reality is shaped hierarchically, as in Dante's vision, with a Supreme Being (God), angels, humans, animals, vegetative life, and so on. In the traditional Christian view, Christ occupies the axial position between God the Creator and humanity. As Milosz said, "the Descent of God and the Ascension are two of the spatial poles without which religion becomes pure spirituality devoid of any toehold in reality, a situation *not to man's measure*" (223; emphasis added). The notion of hierarchy is crucial to the questions of order and value, and here Milosz affirms his belief that the historical event that defines human nature, order, and value in the world in the fullest sense is the incarnation, death, and bodily resurrection of Jesus.

Milosz's insight into the radical shift from belief in man as a metaphysical creature to belief in "historical man" sheds light on Heaney's relationship to the Northern Ireland Catholicism of his youth. As a child and young adult, he grew up in and experienced this radical shift. As he indicated to Karl Miller, "my own personal experience mirrors that and is part of it" (36). As his consciousness developed, he came to question the cultural Catholicism of the Derry world, especially insofar as that conventional belief was bound up with the nationalist political and military struggle against Protestant Unionists. Early poems like "Casualty" and "Punishment" reveal his anguished and ambivalent relation to the situation, bound to the community yet distancing himself from the nationalist pieties and tribal rituals. This is not to say, however, that Heaney abandoned belief in "metaphysical man." Far from it. Rather, his mature view evolved into one that much resembles that expressed by Milosz in his manifesto titled "Essay in Which the Author Confesses. . . ." (2001, 233–45). Milosz (and Weil) defines man's metaphysical being, his inherent drive for freedom and transcendence, as "the divine in man" pushing against the pervasive historicist viewpoint, the deterministic view of man as strictly a creature of history and nature (i.e., Necessity). Milosz associates "the divine in man" with the force of light, which is a key image throughout Heaney's poetry. Milosz asks: "What, then, is the light? The divine in man turning against the natural in him—in other words, intelligence dissenting from 'meaninglessness,' searching for meaning, grafted onto darkness like a noble shoot onto a wild tree, growing greater and stronger only in and through man" (238). The personal struggle, then, is to exercise freedom and develop a more self-conscious identity by resisting the cultural, political, and religious forces that frustrate and limit that drive for autonomy and individuation, the spiritual basis for which is man's metaphysical nature. This is exactly what Heaney set out to do, and it has profoundly complicated his relationship to the Derry community of cultural Catholicism, creating a tension between his ties to "home," to the larger world beyond Ireland, *and* to the transcendent order.

Several critics and in fact Heaney himself have pointed to the writings of Carl Jung as an important influence on Heaney's personal and poetic struggle for greater self-consciousness and individuation.[1] In his classic study *Modern*

Man in Search of A Soul (ca. 1950), Jung described "the modern spiritual problem" and the individual's struggle for greater self-consciousness and autonomy (196–221). Jung stated that "modern man has lost all the metaphysical certainties of his medieval brother," replacing them with "the ideals of material security, general welfare and humaneness" (204). Jung found these humanistic goals inadequate for the needs of the soul. Having lost his roots in the past, modern man is now "unhistorical" and self-conscious and, therefore, "guilty" and "solitary" (198–99). Nevertheless, Jung believed that by facing this predicament honestly and struggling through it, the individual can achieve a higher consciousness and greater integration of his or her personality; he or she can find a greater measure of self-transcendence and discover "new forms of life" (217).

However, Jung conceives of transcendence as only a psychological phenomenon. He denied the existence of a metaphysical order, a reality independent of human construction. For him, the notion of a metaphysical dimension is itself only a psychic "projection" of past ages, which has now become meaningless. His idea of transcendence is strictly of a mundane phenomenon (what Milosz would call an aspect of "historical man"), without any basis in a real order of being. Jung affirms the reality of "the soul" against the modern age's various determinisms (e.g., consumerism, collectivism, etc.), but it is "soul" understood as a psychic rather than spiritual entity. Criticizing Jung's claims, theologian Martin Buber spoke precisely to this point:

> He (Jung) explains that God does not exist independent of the human subject. The controversial question is therefore this: Is God merely a psychic phenomenon or does He also exist independently of the psyche of man? Jung answers, God does not exist for Himself. One can also state the question in this way: Does that which the man of faith calls divine action (i.e. grace) arise merely from his own inner self or can the action of a super-psychic Being also be included in it? Jung answers that it arises from one's inner self. (1952, 78–96)

The argument is crucial, and indeed problematic, for grasping Heaney's struggle to understand his own development. On the one hand, Heaney has affirmed Jung's importance for his own drive toward higher consciousness, his personal effort to individuate himself and transcend the cramping influences of his upbringing within Derry Catholic culture. On the other hand, as we saw, he has acknowledged the importance of his early Catholic training—training in the doctrines of eternity, the soul, the sacraments, the mystical body, and the Creator's "attentiveness" to one's "inmost thoughts"—as relevant to his development as a poet. But the Jungian and Catholic views are essentially incompatible, since unlike Milosz, Weil, and, I believe, Heaney, Jung does not allow for any independent metaphysical reality. Since Jung sees man as essentially a historical being, transcendence for him is intermundane. But for Milosz and Weil, the "divine in man" is grounded in a supernatural source that makes possible some liberation from necessity in history. Heaney, while acknowledging his debt to Jung, comes closer to the thought of Milosz and Weil, as we shall see. Moreover, all of the essentials of Catholic teaching Heaney enumerated as important influences in his formation are focused within history in the doctrine of Jesus's incarnation and bodily resurrection—God entering history—and derive their meaning from that event. The belief in Jesus as the Son of God who became man, died, and rose from the dead validates metaphysical man, the infinite sacredness, and worth of the individual. It validates human freedom and imbues the drive for transcendence and ethical responsibility with the highest possible, i.e., eternal, significance.

In brief, Heaney's statements about the influence of his Catholic teaching and about poetry as grace presuppose the doctrine of Jesus's incarnation and resurrection. His statements are finally incomprehensible without that doctrine. That central Catholic doctrine, mysterious as it is, gives transcendence "a toehold in reality" against the gnosis of pure spirituality, and it is "fit to man's measure," as Milosz said (2001, 223). Christian transcendence is not a Gnostic flight from the gravity of history but rather a process of transfiguring the self within the particularities of time and place. Because Jung reduces the notion of transcendence to a psychic reality, Buber finds him to be ultimately a Gnostic in his thinking. Heaney the poet is not a Gnostic. One way to view his poetry is as a record of his struggle to express the dynamic process of individuation and heightened consciousness, a la Jung, yet also to express in new ways the mysterious transcendent dimensions of reality, a key source of which is his early Catholic training. Like Milosz's, Heaney's religious search in his poems takes the form of "intelligence dissenting from 'meaninglessness,' searching for meaning, grafted onto darkness like a noble shoot on a wild tree," signified by "light, grace, the love of the Good" (Milosz 2001, 238).

Many of Heaney's early poems, such as "Limbo," "The Cleric," "The Scribes," "The Master," and especially "Station Island," reveal his critical questioning and restiveness under the gravitational weight of the conventional Catholicism of his youth. In the early poem "Limbo," for example, he examines the traditional Catholic notion of Limbo as it might be applied to the eternal destiny of a baby drowned by a shamed mother who "waded in under / The sign of her cross." The unbaptized victim, according to Catholic belief, will be deprived of heaven, left forever unredeemed in Limbo where "Even Christ's palms, unhealed, smart and cannot fish there" (1972, 70). The shamed mother, the poem implies, is a victim weighed down by the gravity of a pharisaical Catholicism that brands both the "fallen woman" and her child as outcasts. Seeking freedom from such a stunting ideology, the poet in "Station Island" undertakes a spiritual journey in which, unlike Dante, he discovers and defines his artistic identity by rejecting cultural Catholicism, though not without some measure of guilt at the separation. As the ghost of James Joyce tells him:

> Your obligation
> is not discharged by any common rite
> What you do you must do on your own. . . .
> Let go, let fly, forget
> You've listened long enough. Now strike your note. (1998, 245)

Heaney's growing self-consciousness and individuation, his increasingly angular stance toward the cultural Catholicism of his youth, was perhaps best expressed in the final poem of *Wintering Out* (1972), "Westering." Looking back at Ireland from his vantage point in California, the poet recalls the beginning of his journey to America from Donegal on Good Friday, when he drove past churches filled with "congregations bent / To the studded crucifix" (25–26). He asks: "What nails dropped out that hour?" thinking perhaps of the contradiction between the believers' ritual piety and their role in the daily rituals of sectarian murder and passive acquiescence. Now living six thousand miles from the insular convention-bound communities of Northern Ireland, the poet can imagine "untroubled dust / a loosening gravity"—peace and reconciliation—but only as an optative wish. The reality at home in Derry is otherwise, where the poet finds no hint of reconciliation. Unlike in John Donne's "Good Friday: Riding Westward," the poem it imitates, no communal redemption is imagined here. In "Westering," Christ the mediator still hangs suspended on the cross, "weighing by his hands." So, too, is the poet himself. Though he has left the "still churches" behind, he remains suspended like Christ in a state of "free fall," beyond the communal pieties of home but also weighed down by the guilt of his own ambiguous freedom. He is still anchored to "home" by memory and by communal and familial ties, yet also more distant and free. In particular, he is freer because he has achieved a poetic self-consciousness that enables him in some measure to transcend the past through the transformative power of language.

In the Miller interview, as we saw, Heaney dated his rediscovery of the language and meaning of his early Catholic tradition as occurring after the death of his parents. But long before that rediscovery, as "Limbo," "Westering," and other poems reveal, Heaney was already examining, challenging, and transforming the language and meaning of that Catholic tradition as part of his expanding poetic vision. A more subtle transformation of doctrine and language can be seen in "Settings xxi" from *Seeing Things* (1991), where he describes the impact of firing a rifle at a white cloth target by comparing it to an invigorating shock to the soul, one that is paradoxically both a personal "fall" into sin and a discovery of language's meaning and force:

> Once and only once I fired a gun—
> A .22. At a square of handkerchief
> Pinned on a tree about sixty yards away.
>
> It exhilarated me—the bullet's song
> So effortlessly at my fingertip,
> The target's single shocking little jerk,
>
> A whole new quickened sense of what *rifle* meant.
> And then again as it was in the beginning
> I saw the soul like a white cloth snatched away
>
> Across dark galaxies and felt that shot
> For the sin it was against eternal life—
> Another phrase dilating in new light. (17)

Here, Heaney transforms conventional religious concepts and language ("in the beginning," "the soul," "sin . . . against eternal life") by concentrating them on the personal shock of having gratuitously violated the order of the universe, so that now the phrases' meanings are revealed "in new light." Act ("shooting"), word ("rifle"), and effect ("sin") coalesce in a dynamic triad that encompasses creation: "In the beginning" (was the Word), transgression, loss of innocence, fall, and fresh knowledge "in new light" (addition mine). For the speaker, the real subject of the poem becomes the mysteriously dynamic relation between words, actions, and understanding. His "sin," he discovers, is not merely some harmless boyhood act but an assertion of the personal ego against the eternal order of things. Though the act of shooting is simple, it echoes the original sin that reverberated throughout the universe. At the same time, the discovery of language and meaning are an experience of self-knowledge and growth.

In the subsequent poem, "Settings xxii," the speaker probes the mystery of incarnate spirit:

> Where does spirit live? Inside or outside
> Things remembered, made things, things unmade? How habitable is perfected
>   form?
> And how habitable the windy light?

The question the poet asks is: How does spirit interpenetrate the actual world and the human mind? What is the relationship between the invisible force of light and the visible world? One answer is suggested in the second section of the title poem, "Seeing Things," where the speaker, like Joyce's Stephen Dedalus, examines the meaning of the term "Claritas" (quiddity, whatness) by intuiting the movement of spirit reflected in a cathedral sculpture depicting the baptism of Jesus:

> *Claritas.* The dry-eyed Latin word
> Is perfect for the carved stone of the water
> Where Jesus stands up to his unwet knees
> And John the Baptist pours out more water
> Over his head: all this in bright sunlight
> On the façade of a cathedral. Lines
> Hard and thin and sinuous represent
> The flowing river. Down between the lines
> Little antic fish are all go. Nothing else.
> And yet in that utter visibility
> The stone's alive with what's invisible. (lines 23–38, Heaney 1998, 316–17)

These examples from *Seeing Things* and the earlier *Wintering Out* show something of the complexity of Heaney's ongoing relation as a poet to the Christian tradition. They reveal a consciousness ready to challenge and reassess—though not completely abandon—his cultural religious inheritance and ready to make it a subject of imaginative transformation in his poetry. To the extent that he does this, Heaney keeps a firm foothold in both the historical milieu and in the vertical, transcendent dimension of reality he learned in his early Catholic training, and in so doing he resists being encapsulated within a purely historical-cultural framework.

Moreover, in addition to acknowledging the importance of his Catholic training for his poetry, Heaney has criticized the "hermeneutic of suspicion" fostered by the school of deconstruction in much contemporary literary analysis, a hermeneutic fundamentally at odds with Christian realism. In his conversation with Miller, he defended traditional critical approaches and the literary values they hold to because "they embodied a morality, an ethics. To give up the old style of literary criticism, to embrace deconstruction—that breaks all sorts of covenants" (Miller 2000, 46). Apropos Heaney's argument, Milosz believed that the ethical covenant's ultimate source is the "covenant with God [that] allows man to disengage himself from the net of immutable laws binding creation" (2001, 238). For Milosz, the covenant with God is manifested in history in the Hebrew and Christian traditions of the covenant of the Word and especially for Christians in the Word-made-flesh in Jesus and the Gospels (320). While Heaney's remark does not explicitly link the ethical/literary covenant to theology, his disavowal of deconstruction's premises makes clear his belief in a "covenant" or community of meaning rooted in a shared understanding of words as the basis for ethical order in society and for ethical meaning in literature, a bond that is transgenerational, transnational, and ultimately transhistorical.

Heaney's attitude toward the covenant of language is captured in the opening section of "On His Work in the English Tongue":

> Post-this, post-that, post-the-other, yet in the end
> Not past a thing. Not understanding or telling
> Or forgiveness.
>   But often past oneself,
> Pounded like a shore by the roller griefs
> In language that can still knock language sideways. (lines 1–6, 2001, 73)

Paradoxically, Heaney suggests that language has the power to express what is seemingly beyond our capacities for understanding, telling, and forgiving. In this elegiac tribute to his friend, poet Ted Hughes, he finds the overwhelming grief suffered by King Hrethel in *Beowulf* and the universal language of woe that expresses it to be as true and as timely as ever. And so he concludes:

> Soul has its scruples. Things not to be said.
> Things for keeping, that can keep the small hours gaze
> Open and steady. Things for the *aye* of God
> And for poetry. Which is, as Milosz says,
> "A dividend from ourselves," a tribute paid
> By what we have been true to. A thing allowed. (lines 59–64, 2001, 73–74)

As Milosz and Heaney suggest, a covenant based on a shared understanding of values depends upon some fundamental belief about language—about the source and meaning of words, i.e., the "*aye* of God"—even among deconstructionists and poststructuralists. As many scholars have pointed out, one of the ironies of these latter critical schools is that their promoters argue their cases against language's original authority by using traditionally accepted assumptions about discourse, meaning, and value in order to assert the "truth" of their own often apodictic deconstructive claims about language. Even though in the evolution of language and human consciousness the original simple "covenant" between the word and the world, between sign and signified, has been long broken or is "knocked sideways," a fact Heaney would readily acknowledge, the alternative of complete linguistic relativism, as he suggests, undermines the possibility of truth and the ethical foundations of society. Deconstruction and its offshoots want to answer the basic question of the transcendent source of language and its authority by regarding it as only a sign of the culturally relative logocentric "myth" of origins, a myth that posits a "metaphysics of presence" that deconstructionists deny. In contrast, Heaney's statement affirms a "covenant" of meaning linked to universal human experience, such as King Hrethel's grief, however much language changes. He is, then, a linguistic realist in the tradition of Christian realism, i.e., one who believes "that there is an order of meaning existing *independently* of the structure of any given language that is the foundation for all else" (Ellis 1989, 35).

For Heaney that order of meaning can be approached and suggested through language, despite the labyrinthian permutations of language's historical and cultural evolutions. The relationship between language, the transcendent order, and ordinary human experience is ultimately a mystery, a mystery that is a source of poetic inspiration. His concern in many poems has been with the question of this source of meaning and with the evolution of language, as evidenced by his obsession with etymologies and by his many translations. Often his poems explore the changes language undergoes and the sociopolitical impact of those changes. For example, in his early poem "Toome," he examines the ancient roots of place and place-names and his own personal and poetic "immersion" in such grounding places and their "language":

My mouth holds round
the soft blastings,
Toome, Toome,
as under the dislodged

slab of the tongue
I push into a souterrain
prospecting what new
in a hundred centuries'

loam, flints, musket-balls,
fragmented ware,
torcs and fish-bones
till I am sleeved in

alluvial mud that shelves
suddenly under
bogwater and tributaries,
and elvers tail my hair. (lines 1–16, 1998, 54)

Later, in "At Toomebridge," he retrospectively explores the historical and sociopolitical evolution of the site after the beginning of the peace process in Northern Ireland:

> Where the flat water
> Came pouring over the weir out of Lough Neagh
> As if it had reached an edge of the flat earth
> And fallen shining to the continuous
> Present of the Bann.
>
> Where the checkpoint used to be.
> Where the rebel boy was hanged in '98.
> Where negative ions in the open air
> Are poetry to me. As once before
> The slime and silver of the fattened eel. (lines 1–10, 2001, 3)

Yet in addition to his concern with the historical and sociopolitical dimensions and permutations of language, Heaney also explores the poet's quest to recapture the original experience of language and meaning. A good example of this quest is his translation of the Romanian Marin Sorescu's poem, "The First Words":

> The first words got polluted
> Like river water in the morning
> Flowing with the dirt
> Of blurbs and the front pages.
> My only drink is meaning from the deep brain,
> What the birds and the grass and the stones drink.
> Let everything flow
> Up to the four elements,
> Up to water and earth and fire and air. (lines 1–9, 1996, 47)

The poet's goal, Heaney suggests, is "meaning from the deep brain," that is, the root source of meaning, however "polluted" by the babble of "blurbs" and "front pages." As in Robert Frost's "Directive" and in several of Heaney's poems, this original source is signified by running water, an emblem of the spiritual source of meaning and inspiration in "the deep brain." That source of order and meaning is, for Heaney, transcendent and real. To understand his sense of this transcendent order of meaning, we can recall philosopher Owen Barfield's description of the nature of the "deep brain" in relation to naming, meaning, human consciousness, and the lost world of "first words," a description he derives from the tradition of Christian realism:

That lost world . . . was a world in which both phenomenon and name were felt as representations. On the one hand, "the word conceived in the mind is representative of the whole of that which is realized in thought." . . . But on the other hand the phenomenon itself only achieves full reality (actus) in the moment of being "named" by man; that is, when that in nature which it represents is united with that in man which the name represents. Such naming, however, need not involve vocal utterance. For the name or word is not mere sound, or mere ink. For Aquinas, as for Augustine, there are, anterior to the uttered word, (and) the intellect-word, the heart word and the memory-word (*verbum intellectus, verbum cordis, verbum memoriae*). The human word proceeds from memory, as the Divine Word proceeds from the Father. Proceeds from it, yet remains one with it. For the world is the thought of God realized through His Word. Thus, the Divine Word is *forma exemplaris*; the phenomena are its representations; as the human word is the representation of the *intellectus in actu*. But, once again, the phenomenon itself only achieves its full reality (*actus*) in being named or thought by man; for thinking *is* the thing thought, in act; just as the senses in act, are the thing sensed in act. . . . St. Thomas expressly ratifies the dictum of Aristotle in his *De Anima*, that "the soul is in a manner all things."(1965, 85–86)

Following Aristotle and St. Thomas Aquinas, Barfield expresses the fundamental covenant of language and meaning as having its origin in the divine Logos. Such a belief is the ground of a realistic ontology and is, I believe, the source of Heaney's poetic search for meaning amidst the "pollution" of language so evident in the culture. Many of his poems, like "Toome" and "At Toomebridge," at once move backward in time and memory (*verbum memoriae*) toward the source, in order to move forward toward a greater understanding of our present spiritual condition, especially by calling to mind the original covenant between world and word. As he says in his translation of Sorescu:

Let everything flow
Up to the four elements
Up to water and earth and fire and air.

That this ontology and metaphysical view of language is no longer well regarded by many contemporary thinkers and critics is well-known. It has been largely drowned out by the general wave of linguistic nominalism and cultural relativism. O'Brien's study of Heaney's "alterity" can be seen as typical of many critical responses to literature in our time, where the emphasis is mainly on social issues of gender, race, ethnicity, and class. Popular critical fashion follows the age, but it is an age that many regard as seriously out of balance in its general disregard of such a transcendent and metaphysical dimension. Heaney, as we shall see, is a writer like W. B. Yeats, Václav Havel, Czeslaw Milosz, T. S. Eliot, Simone Weil, and others, one who is deeply aware of this imbalance and who struggles to redress it by evoking a transcendent ideal in his poetry.

As this introduction suggests, my study is not a work of literary analysis in the strictly academic sense. Neither is it a study of the influence of Weil on Heaney per se. I plan to analyze the way in which Heaney the Irish poet and Weil the French mystic philosopher work to redress the "imbalance" of the twentieth century by affirming an ideal reality by which to measure the present times and suggest an alternative and truer mode of vision and action. My study was initially inspired by my discovery of the many correspondences in thought and feeling between Weil's *Gravity and Grace* (1947, in English, 1952,) and Heaney's *The Spirit Level* (1996). In that volume and in other poems, as I shall illustrate, Heaney employs concepts of gravity and grace (light), of counterweighing and balancing, as principles to construct the form and meaning of most of the poems. These principles, which govern both theme and poetic strategy, are rooted in his metaphysical vision. While they have been an important feature of his poetic strategy at least since *The Haw Lantern*, in *The Spirit Level* they achieve an unmistakable preeminence and fulfillment. Despite the obvious and considerable differences between Heaney and Weil, who died before Heaney's poetic career was underway, there are remarkable affinities between their metaphysical and ethical perspectives, their understanding of the age, and their belief in the ethical power of art to counterbalance the age's distortions and excesses. At the same time, there are important differences between Heaney and Weil that I shall explore, especially their views on the role of imagination in the human effort to reshape and transcend actual circumstances.

In chapter 1 I shall examine Weil's philosophic response to the "unbalanced" age and her search for transcendence through spiritual discipline. In chapter 2 I shall examine Heaney's respond to the "unbalanced" age in his search for meaning and transcendence as a poet. In chapter 3 I shall explore how Heaney's poetry, primarily in *The Spirit Level*, is shaped in response to the fundamental principles expressed in Weil's *Gravity and Grace*. A study of these two writers, linked by their mutual relation to Milosz, helps us to understand some of the profound spiritual questions facing the age by showing how Heaney and Weil confront these questions and offer a salutary vision by focusing on the axis point where mundane and transcendent coordinates intersect, where gravity and grace interpenetrate.

1

SIMONE WEIL AND THE
AGE OF IMBALANCE

Before turning to examine in detail Heaney's relation to Weil, his aesthetic, and his poetry, it is important to recall Weil's fundamental response to the age. What is the nature of the imbalance that Weil and Heaney perceive in modern Western culture? In the deepest sense, it is the corruption and radical distortion of the sense of *meaning* and *value* throughout the culture. This imbalance is caused by the loss or threatened loss of belief in the transcendent spiritual order, or what Heaney calls "the glimpsed ideal." Man is now regarded only as "historical man," as Milosz said. The imbalance is manifested on all levels—metaphysical, social, political, and ethical—and is at the heart of the chaotic events witnessed in the twentieth century. Viewing post–World War I European society, Weil put the matter succinctly: "Outside the sphere of external observances (bourgeois formality) the whole moral trend of the post-war years (and even before) has been an *apology* for *intemperance* and therefore, ultimately, for madness" (Panichas 1977, xxx). Despite lip service to the democratic ideal of justice and equality, relations of naked power and self-interest dominate the political and social orders. In particular, Weil pointed to the forces of collectivism under technocracy and the dehumanization of work as especially destructive of the human spirit and individual freedom. "The conditions of modern life destroy the mind-body equilibrium in everything—in thought and action—in all actions. The civilization we live in overwhelms the human *body*. Man and body have become strangers to one another. Content has been lost." Humanism, she contended, "was not wrong in thinking that truth, beauty, equality are of infinite worth, but in thinking that man can obtain them for himself without grace." Weil concluded:

19

"We no longer know how to receive grace" (xxix–xxxi). The result, for Weil, is a society that has lost its spiritual moorings in the transcendent order, for her the ultimate source of grace. Consequently, under the pressure of the culture's domination by technology and reductive rationalism, our sense of the metaphysical order has shrunk to the point where the individual's very humanity is radically diminished or lost. Man has become or is in danger of becoming a "thing," a slave to the forces of gravity. Weil believed that citizens in "advanced" Western societies suffer what philosopher Eric Voegelin called a "deformation of being," a condition that dominates the social order and, increasingly, modern consciousness.[2]

To further clarify Weil's sense of the situation, we can recall her basic anthropology. For her, man is a metaphysical unity of spirit and matter, a being constituted *by nature* to seek his ultimate meaning in the transcendent good. His value as a creature is defined by that end. He lives in the *metaxu*, i.e., between the transcendent and the earthly. Yet this metaphysical view of man has been largely denied or subverted in modern Western culture. However, as Milosz and Flannery O'Connor pointed out, the age is not atheological (Milosz 2001, 246; O'Connor 1969, 33, 47, 67). Rather, it is governed by a Manichean spirit. At one extreme the weight of rationalism, positivism, and materialism threatens to reduce all reality to the various determinisms currently ruling society. At the other extreme, man's theological impulse, now loosed from its existential anchor in the concrete world, becomes vaporized in Gnostic flights from the real. In this neo-Manichean ethos, the religious impulse is displaced into the many Gnostic "isms"—Nazism, communism, humanism—that propose to create through human effort alone an earthly paradise of freedom, justice, and self-fulfillment but without reference to the transcendent order and without grace. These efforts continually issue in failure and despair. More disastrously, for Weil, the very meaning and value of the individual is lost. This is why Milosz said that Weil's attention was focused on "the central problem of recovering the notion of the human" (2001, 216).

Of course many writers besides Weil, Milosz, and O'Connor have pointed to the age's imbalance. In *Poetry, Language and Thought* Martin Heidegger spoke of the loss of the spiritual dimension of things in a technological age where human reason becomes the universal criterion for determining what is "real" (Baker 2005, 165–67). Alfred North Whitehead famously described the imbalance as a "displacement of the real," the real understood to include the metaphysical dimension (1925, 64–82). Several other writers have pointed to the dominance of scientism—the ideology that claims that a rational scientific vision is the sole criterion for reality—as a manifestation of this imbalance and displacement. Philosopher Eric Voegelin described the ethos of scientism as upholding three main dogmas:

1. the assumption that the mathematized science of phenomena is a model science to which all other sciences ought to conform;
2. that all realms of being are accessible to the methods of the sciences of phenomena; and
3. that all reality that is not accessible to the sciences is either irrelevant or, in a more radical form of the dogma, illusory (2000, 168–69).

On a similar note, American novelist Walker Percy named scientism as the dominant ideology in a technological society and argued that this ideology has so saturated modern consciousness that it presumes to define all sectors of reality, completely excluding the spiritual:

> The question is not whether the Good News is no longer relevant, but rather whether it is possible that man is currently undergoing a tempestu-ous restructuring of his consciousness which does not presently allow him to take account of the Good News. For what has happened is not merely the technological transformation of the world but something psychologically even more portentous. It is the absorption by the layman not of the scien-tific method but rather of the mystical aura of science, whose credentials he accepts for all sectors of reality. . . . Such a man could not take account of God, the devil, and the angels if they were standing before him, because he has already peopled the universe with his own hierarchies.[3]

Speaking of the "presumption of reason" and scientism's dubious triumph, Milosz echoed Percy and asked: "is it not then fair to recognize the error and to concede with humility that the disappearance of the very substance of man shows us the overly high price we have paid for this progress of sci-ence?" (2001, 214). Lacking belief in the metaphysical order, man is reduced to a historical being, whom Milosz described as being "like a fly trapped in amber, a being viewed entirely as a creature defined by historical events and circumstances" (251). His view was shared by Weil, who believed that modernity's "science-inspired" viewpoint is responsible for "a degradation of our thought and thus our conception of the world in which we live" (Spring-sted 1983, 233). Scientism's dominance, she said, is nearly total: "so far as the prestige of science is concerned, there are no such people now who are unbelievers . . . (it) has led us to believe that force reigns supreme over all phenomena, contrary to the need for justice in human relations" (233–34). Yet as Milosz argued, rational scientism cannot finally account for the mys-tery of human nature and human consciousness: "Man cannot be reduced to just a part of history; history is unable to produce a moral judgment unless we ascribe magical qualities to it" (2001, 215). Against scientism's hegemony, the aspirations of the human spirit of freedom constantly assert themselves, seen especially in the work of the creative artist. Our very nature as creatures of spirit who live in the *metaxu* and who long for transcendence urges us to rise above purely historical conditions.

To explore in greater detail Weil's reaction against the science-dominated age, I want to focus initially on some basic elements in her metaphysics and theology. As all commentators have acknowledged, her essential vision is grounded in paradox and contradiction. Nevertheless, its central features can be elucidated. At the center of her vision is the concept of *gravity*, which as we shall see is a major theme in Heaney's later poetry. For Weil, gravity is both a physical law and a natural spiritual force: "all the *natural* movements of the soul are controlled by laws analogous to those of physical gravity. Grace is the only exception" (1997, 45). Gravity is the universal condition brought about by God's withdrawal from the world at Creation. But at the same time, as we shall see, Weil believed that God's "presence" is evident in the universe's beauty and order. Her close friend and editor, Gustave Thibon, explained her concept of gravity:

> The central law of the world, from which God has withdrawn by his very act of creation, is the law of gravity, which is to be found analogously at every stage of creation. Gravity is the force which above all others draws us from God. It impels each creature to seek everything which can preserve and enlarge it and, as Thucydides said, to exercise all the power of which it is capable. Psychologically it is shown by all those motives which are directed toward asserting or reinstating the self, by all those secret subterfuges (lies of the inner life, escape in dreams or false ideals, imaginary encroachments on the past and future, etc.) which we make use of to bolster up from inside our tottering existence, that is to say, remain apart from and opposed to God. (20)

For Weil the physical law of gravity is symbolic of man's love of power, a malign force that undermines all sense of proportion and equilibrium and propels him toward baseness and evil (Panichas 1977, xxx). As Weil said, "When, however, a man turns away from God, he simply gives himself up to the law of gravity. Then he thinks that he can decide and choose, but he is only a thing, a stone that falls. If we examine human society and souls closely and with real attention, we see that wherever the virtue of supernatural light is absent, everything is obedient to mechanical laws as blind and as exact as the laws of gravitation."[4] This is why Weil called obedience to gravity "the greatest sin." Weil's historical perspective enabled her to trace the etiology of gravity as brute power from the ancient classical world (e.g. Homer's *The Iliad*) through imperial Rome to twentieth-century totalitarian regimes.[5]

Is there any available counterforce to gravity? Again, Milosz posed the central questions: "Is there an imminent force located in *le devinir*, in what is the state of becoming, a force that pulls mankind up toward perfection? Is there any *cooperation* between man and a universe that is subject to constant change?" (2001, 247–48). Stated differently, Milosz asks whether and to what extent is grace an imminent reality. Weil's answer is that grace is a real possibility and the only adequate counterforce to gravity. Grace is a mystery, an element in man's "contradictory" status as a creature, yet that very contradiction is "the lever of transcendence." (Given the age's imbalance, however, the paradoxical movement of transcendence is toward a recovery of the genuinely human self. In short, the movement of grace is an incarnational movement.) Human reason cannot fully penetrate the mystery; as Milosz observed, "those who believe the contradiction between necessity and the good can be solved on any level other than that of mystery delude themselves" (254–55). However, Weil maintained that, through attention and humility, we can apprehend this mystery *qua* mystery and "judge of the suitability of the words which express it" (1997, 185).

Grace as a supernatural force is represented by "light," a central image throughout Heaney's poetry—light in the double sense of denoting illumination, seeing, and vision, and as denoting weightlessness and lightness, the counter image to gravity. Speaking of the power of gravity, Weil said: "There is only one remedy for that: a chlorophyll conferring the faculty of feeding on light. There is only one fault: incapacity to feed upon light, for where capacity to do this has been lost all faults are possible" (47). Ultimately, for Weil, light (grace) is a manifestation of divine love. "To love God through and across the destruction of Troy and Carthage—and with no consolation. Love is not consolation, it is light" (59).

Nevertheless, Weil's dichotomizing of gravity and grace and her strong emphasis on submission to necessity has suggested to Milosz and others that her outlook was basically that of a Manichean. Her editor Gustave Thibon pinpointed the problem:

> It is significant to note that Simone Weil extends the determinism of Descartes and Spinoza to *all natural* phenomena, including the facts of psychology. Gravity for her is only held in check by grace. She thus overlooks the margin of indetermination and "spontaneity" which God has left in nature and which allows for the introduction of liberty and miracles in the world.

It remains nonetheless true that *in fact* gravity is practically all-powerful:
St. Thomas recognizes that most human actions are prompted by the blind
appetite of the senses and subject to the determination of the stars. (157)

Against this view, critics such as Eric O. Springsted and Tom Werge argue that
her vision, especially her vision of art, is more incarnational and sacramental
than Manichean. For example, Springsted claims that "rather than being a
metaphysical dualist as some commentators have complained, Weil instead
holds to a 'monistic mystery,' and that 'mystery holds the world together.'"[6]
Along similar lines, Werge argues that despite Weil's emphasis on necessity
and on the need for spiritual detachment from the world, her stress on submission to gravity as the path by which we ascend to the good reveals a "sacramental tension" in her metaphysics that shaped her ethics and her view of
art."[7] As we shall see, this problematical issue is crucial when examining her
views on the metaxu, on the role of imagination, and on beauty in art, especially in relation to Heaney's aesthetic and poetic practice.

Weil attempted to bridge the gap between gravity and grace by affirming
man as a creature who by nature inhabits the metaxu in between the transcendent and the earthly. As Springsted has explained, "metaxu" is a Greek adverb
meaning "intermediary," a term Weil used as a noun to describe the human
situation (Springsted 1983, 197–219). The metaxu—earthly realities such as
nature, family, tradition, and culture—serve as bridges to the transcendent.
They are necessary for man's spiritual progress toward the ultimate goal—a
return to God through grace. However, the metaxu are not unequivocally
good. On the one hand, they can serve as intermediary objects of attention
that in turn direct our attention toward God. But on the other hand, they
can become distractions or idols that focus all attention and desire on the
object itself, obscuring its true mediating role. Therefore the crucial point for
spiritual progress is how the metaxu are perceived and used.

For Weil the metaxu can draw the soul toward God, because they are not
simply objects but are "a *representation* made up of the object's influence on
the subject and the medium of the *knowing* subject's own mode of thought.
An object is only efficacious as a (metaxu) for the subject when it is related to
the subject's own *attention*" (199; emphasis added). How is the object related
to the subject's attention? J. M. Baker points out that there is a "*structural*
relationship encompassing subject and object alike"; that is, they are both
metaphysical entities. Therefore, ideally the metaxu both command attention
and direct it, through desire, to the transcendent good (2005, 78; emphasis
added). Weil stated in her *Notebooks*: "[Metaxu] every representation which
draws us toward the non-representable. Need for [metaxu] in order to prevent

us from seizing hold of nothingness instead of full being" (1970, in Spring-sted 1983, 199). The metaxu reflect the "supernatural light" and draw the soul toward the ultimate good.

Since the metaxu, given proper attention, reflect "supernatural light" or grace, they are bridges *from* the transcendent as well as to it. In fact, they can only be the latter because they are the former first. Man's soul is constituted by nature to love and desire the transcendent good. Weil voiced this idea clearly when she prayed, "may my soul be for the body and God only what this penholder is for my hand and the paper—an intermediary" (1970, 132). As vehicles of light, the metaxu can be instruments of grace to help overcome gravity. They could not have this capability of overcoming gravity, however, unless by some means they were conveyors or assistants of grace. They can also serve as "the very means of communication through the mediation of world order," but this is only possible "where there is a descending grace which provides for this order." Paradoxically, grace "operates, not by ignoring gravity or necessity, but by consenting to it" (Springstead 1983, 202–3).

Weil's concept of the metaxu and mediation is of course rooted in her Platonic idealism. But she went on to focus mediation more specifically in Jesus's crucifixion and death. Behind this lay Weil's complicated relation-ship to Judaism and Christianity. Though born a Jew, she rejected Judaism as one of the "great beasts" of civilization (Nevin 1991, 273). At the same time, though strongly attracted to Catholicism's theology of redemption, the sacraments, and the church as the repository of "truth," she condemned its institutional power and its triumphalism as another "great beast" of history. As has been noted, for the most part she ignored the doctrine of Jesus's res-urrection and vehemently rejected the doctrine of the mystical body (273). She believed in the real presence of Christ in the Eucharist but refused the sacraments. Nevertheless, much of her life was devoted to developing her heterodox theology of the cross based on her vision of Jesus as the suffering slave. Salvation through suffering, self-denial, "decreation," and openness to grace in experience of the "void" were the core of her paradoxical belief. In her personal life Weil was driven to live out a self-sacrificing role fashioned on her model of Christ as the exemplary victim.

As Eric O. Springsted noted, for Weil "it is Christ's mediating love as a man in affliction—as one in absolute need—for the Father which provides the primordial means for man to come into contact with God and partici-pate in His life" (1983, 209). By renouncing his divine identity and consent-ing out of love to the most extreme form of gravity—death—Christ became the central mediator of all forms of mediation between God and mankind.

Hence, for Weil "the cross is the lever of transcendence." Christ is the model for renouncing the egoistic self and "descending" into the world's gravities in order, with grace, to rise to the transcendent good. All other intermediaries or metaxu become subsumed under Christ's self-emptying sacrificial act. It represents the ideal of love that measures all relations between the soul and "the world." Given her Platonized Christocentric view, the iron laws of gravity can be transformed from a relation of necessity into a spiritual relation wherein the metaxu become the very means of grace and transcendence. This possible transformation refers not only to those conditions which must be suffered through but also to those experiences of the beauty of earthly things in nature and art that are "lights" (grace) reflecting the truth of the divine order. These two—suffering and beauty—can be instruments of transcendence, a key for understanding her view of the role of art and poetry in the soul's progress.

Nevertheless, Weil's view of the metaxu as grace is skewed by her dismissal of the doctrine of Jesus's bodily resurrection. Christ on the cross is her exemplary model, a heroic spiritual figure. But his role in the ongoing process of mediation and grace has no real theological foundation without belief in Jesus's resurrection. The latter doctrine affirms the glorified bodily Christ as the exemplum and final goal of human existence. Without that belief, Weil's theology is tilted toward dualism and determinism, toward pessimism and self-denial that threatens to undercut the full meaning of man's possible redemption affirmed in Christ's resurrection, as well as the abiding power of the Holy Spirit.

Nevertheless, Weil's concept of the metaxu extends beyond the individual's relation to God through its ethical dimension. It applies to social relations as well and commands a Christian response to others. In *The Need for Roots* she focused on the nature of obligation, that is, each person's duty to respect and help his fellow man in need. Once again, Christ is the model, as when he said "I was hungry and you gave me food" (Matt 25:35). Viewed in ethical terms, earthly needs are the medium through which the metaxu are manifested and obligation fulfilled. As Nevin points out, Weil "argues that the issue of justice is indissolubly bound to and identical with the demands of love." While this demand may seem unreasonable, "there must be moments when from reason's mundane perspective the folly of love is alone reasonable. This folly of love requires compassion for the enemy . . . but what it chiefly solicits is love's free consent as the indispensable mechanism of justice within any society or between individuals" (1991, 314–15). Fulfilling obligation is a matter of justice, but justice based on the transcendent order. As her friend and biographer Simone Pétrement wrote:

Simone believed that justice in society depends on this faith (i.e. in the transcendent good). If one does not understand that the true good is a reality located outside the world which cannot be reached by human faculties but toward which all men possess the power to turn, one cannot, in her opinion, behave justly with human beings. The politics of justice cannot be separated from religion, or, rather from mysticism. (1976, 500)

Weil's view of the metaxu also shaped her understanding of the artist and his art. For her, the work of art is a metaxu and, like all creation, is fundamentally paradoxical. It both commands our attention in itself and simultaneously points to the transcendent reality beyond. It is a finite, transitory object, but it contains traces of the infinite and eternal to which the audience intuitively responds because of an intrinsic correspondence between the art work and human nature. Weil said: "man cannot get over regretting that he has not been given the infinite, and he has more than one way of fabricating, with the finite, an equivalent of the infinite for himself—which is perhaps the definition of art" (Baker 2005, 74). According to J. M. Baker, for Weil every great work of art necessarily manifests human longing, or nostalgia, for the infinite, and what she calls "the moment of nostalgia in the relation of temporal things to the spiritual is something *structural* to material being" (emphasis added). In the recursive "moment of nostalgia," when we apprehend the work of art, "earthly things fulfill their being" as metaxu or bridges to the infinite (75). The artist's task, then, is to "decreate" the subjective self to a degree that enables him to achieve that "higher, strictly impersonal level of consciousness" where "seeing clearly is knowing not only what one sees but also the structure of one's perceptions" (79). As we shall see, her view is remarkably similar to Heaney's argument, via Jung, about the poet's need to "outgrow" the subjective ego and develop objective self-consciousness. For the artist to achieve this level of consciousness is, for Weil, to be able to manifest "the sense of the beautiful that arises from the free contemplation of things" (78). If it achieves this, the work of art as metaxu serves as both a "stopping point" (or to use Heaney's phrase, a "stepping stone") for beauty and appreciation as well as a medium of "passage" to the transcendent.

A more problematic issue in Weil's aesthetic concerns her view of imagination, especially when considered in relation to Heaney the poet. Once again, her view is complex and paradoxical. Many of her statements suggest that she regarded imagination negatively as a function of the subjective ego, which must undergo decreation. For example, she said: "Man has to perform an act of incarnation, for he is disembodied (*disincarne*) by his imagination. What comes to us from Satan is our imagination" (1997, 103). Imagination is evil because it produces illusion and "a false infinitude." Because of God's

absence in a world governed by necessity, imagination fills the void by pro-
ducing idols that delude us with false hopes and desires. In her view, imagination is contrary to contemplation (Nevin 1991, 156, 283).

Here, Weil is considering imagination from the standpoint of her ascetic
morality regarding the soul's striving for the ultimate good. As ascetic disci-
plinarian, she rejected imagination as a distraction from the essential work
of decreating the self as a precondition for receiving grace and for transcendence. As Thibon remarked, in Weil's view:

> We must accept emptiness, an unequal balance, we must never seek compen-
> sation and, above all, we must suspend the work of our imagination "which
> perpetually tends to stop up the cracks through which grace flows . . . " we
> must renounce the past and the future. . . . Memory and hope destroy the
> wholesome effect of affliction by providing an unlimited field where we can
> be lifted up in imagination ("I used to be, I shall be"). (Weil 1997, 21)

But as Nevin points out, Weil "is taking a moral (moralistic) position against
imagination. It is evil, she contends, in persuading us that the final good may
be secured in the world and so it prompts us to betray that good by creating attachments." But she also argued that "the beauty of the highest art, on
the contrary, has a quality of nakedness; it is unshrouded by imagination
and thus affords us God's presence. It is 'reality without attachment'" (1991,
157). Thus in speaking of the effect of great art on the audience, Weil paradoxically maintained that "the beautiful is the carnal attraction which keeps
us at a distance and implies a renunciation. This implies the renunciation
of that which is most deep-seated, the imagination" (Weil 1997, 205). She
believed there is a danger that imagination will distract the audience from the
mystery of the transcendent embedded in the metaxu, because "the imagination has a tendency to universalize what is essentially limited . . . creating
fantasy in the pejorative sense, for it tailors the world to our taste and liking"
(Dunaway and Springsted 1996, 27).

At the same time, Weil also believed that natural beauty and the beauty
of great art are manifestations of God's presence (who is nevertheless *deus
absconditis*). She claimed that "in everything that gives us the pure aesthetic
feeling of beauty there really is the presence of God. There is, as it were,
an incarnation of God in the world and it is indicated by beauty . . . the
beautiful is the experimental proof that the incarnation is possible." While
acknowledging that the beautiful work of art has an author, she also claimed
that "it has something which is essentially anonymous about it. It imitates the
beauty of divine art. In the same way the beauty of the world proves there to
be a God who is personal and impersonal as the same time and is neither the

one nor the other" (1997, 205). Defending her paradoxical position, Springsted argues that her literary creed is inseparable from her religious creed and
that its purpose is to "focus our attention on the mysterious quality of the
redemption by painting it in 'contradictory' terms that show its depth and
uniqueness" (Dunaway and Springsted 1996, 26). In his view, Weil calls for
a literature that can "awaken us to reality" by presenting a vision that is "the
fruit of having paid attention to the world. Attention is the sacrificial suspension of the ego that allows us to see the world as it is and not as we would like
to see it" (28).

Weil's whole aesthetic, her view of beauty and of great art, is rooted in
her view of Jesus's incarnation and death on the cross. She said: "the longing
to love the beauty of the world in a human being is essentially the longing for
the Incarnation" (1951, 171–72). Viewed from an ontological perspective,
the Cross is the intersection of the relation between God and man, between
gravity and grace, between love and beauty. Given this belief, Weil's view of
great art and its beauty is inextricably linked to suffering. Jesus's crucifixion
represents the ultimate submission to gravity, but it is also, mysteriously, a
beautiful manifestation of God's love. As Katherine T. Brueck points out, for
Weil "the whole creation is nothing but the vibration of the harmony created
when Christ continued to love the Father perfectly at the deepest point of his
affliction on the cross. When Jesus cried out to God, 'why hast thou abandoned me?' the perfect, though hidden, love these only apparently despairing
words contain constitutes the secret of both goodness and truth. All forms
of aesthetic beauty, including beautiful art, point in some way to this loving
cry" (Dunaway and Springsted 1996, 111). Thus for Weil Jesus's death on
the cross represents an inner spiritual victory, a paradoxical transcendence
of gravity *through* complete submission to it out of love for the divine Being
and the ultimate harmony of creation. Divine love transfigures suffering into
beauty and joy.

Weil's belief in this incarnation-centered aesthetic owes something to her
personal mystical experience. During Easter Week in 1938, she attended all
the liturgical services at Solesmes. Suffering from a terrible headache, she
reported how she was able "by an extreme effort of concentration . . . to rise
above the wretched flesh, to leave it to suffer by itself, heaped up in a corner,
and to find a pure and perfect joy in the unimaginable beauty of the chanting
and the words." On another occasion, again suffering a severe headache, Weil
memorized and recited George Herbert's poem "Love" like a "prayer" and
reported how during one of her recitations "Christ himself came down and
took possession of me" (Panichas 1977, 7–8). Significantly, Herbert's poem

describes how God, through Christ's sacrifice, absolved the sinner of blame, so that the humbled creature can now "serve" and take communion ("taste my meat") (xliii).

Herbert's poem, viewed in terms of Weil's incarnational spiritual aesthetic, affirms her sense of the dynamic of great art. Speaking of the beauty of created works, she described their dynamics as a "double movement of descent: to do again, out of love, what gravity does: Is not the double movement of descent the key to all art?" The double movement, of course, replicates the incarnation of Jesus. She regarded music as the most transcendent art form and added:

> This movement of descent, the mirror of grace, is the essence of all music. All the rest merely serves to enshrine it. The rising of the notes is a purely sensorial rising. The descent is at the same time a sensorial descent and a spiritual rising. Here we have the paradise which every being longs for: where the slope of nature makes us rise toward the good. (1997, 206)

Commenting on this passage, Thibon added: "*Descendit ad infernos* . . . so in another order, great art redeems gravity by espousing it out of love" (206).

Weil's incarnational aesthetic and its down-up movement ipso facto focuses on the tragic dimension of life and art. Her emphasis is on the mystery of suffering as the key to love. This is understandable, given her almost total disregard of Christ's resurrection. But as J. Huby has pointed out, "the crucifixion and the resurrection are not so much two separate events as one mystery with two facets."[8] Weil focused on Christ's *kenosis* rather than on his glorification, on human tragedy rather than on hope for the world except through total self-emptying to gravity. What saved her from a purely Jansenistic or dualistic vision was her belief, however faint, in the possibilities of grace within the metaxu. Nevertheless, for her the dynamic movement in great art, analogous in form to Christ's movement toward spiritual victory through suffering and death, culminates on Calvary and not at the empty tomb.

Weil's emphasis on George Herbert's poem "Love" as an important influence on her spiritual life and the development of her aesthetic provides a convenient bridge to Heaney because it suggests some analogous lines of thought. In "The Redress of Poetry," Heaney points to Herbert as a prime example of the principle of redressing, and he defines Herbert's poetics in ways substantially applicable to his own later poetry, especially poems in *The Spirit Level*.

Heaney's prime example of this dynamic is Herbert's "The Pulley," a poem about human restlessness in the metaxu, and about the hoped-for ascent to God. It is significant that Heaney would choose "The Pulley" as the main example of his argument for the redress of poetry. Its central formal and thematic tension—up/down, rest/restlessness—exemplifies Heaney's belief in poetry as a "riff" in time that "concentrates consciousness back on itself," as we shall see. In Herbert's poem, the riff focuses the mind directly on the relationship between God and man—God's remoteness on the one hand and His gift of restlessness (desire) on the other, a gift that paradoxically can lead the soul back to God. After God bestows the gift of beauty, wisdom, honor, and pleasure upon man, with only "Rest" remaining, He ruminates:

> For if I should (said he)
> Bestow the jewell also on my creature,
> He would adore my gifts in stead of me,
> And rest in Nature, not the God of Nature:
> So both should losers be.
>
> Yet let him keep the rest,
> But keep them with repining restlessnesse:
> Let him be rich and wearie, that at least,
> If goodnesse lead him not, yet wearinesse
> May tosse him to my breast.[9]

In the poem, restlessness becomes a "lever" of grace that can enable transcendence. In his analysis of the poem, Heaney focuses on the up-down gravitational movement that produces a vital equilibrium "both by the argument and by the rhythm and rhyme." He concludes that "the poem can be read as a mimetic rendering of any pulley-like exchange of forces, but equally it presents itself as an allegory of the relationship between humanity and the God-head, a humanity whose hearts, in St. Augustine's phrase, 'are restless till they rest in Thee'"(1995, 11). Heaney maintains that poems like Herbert's "The Pulley" and "The Collar" are "of present use," because they project both the universal and deeply felt constraints of the gravity of the human predicament and the equally felt hope and aspiration for grace and transcendence. In other words, they embody a metaphysical vision that can also be practically effective. As Heaney said: "when the terrorists sit down at the negotiating table, when the newly independent state enters history still being administered by the old colonial civil service, then the reversal which the poem rehearses is merely being projected upon a more extensive and populous screen" (13–14). Heaney's belief here echoes W. B. Yeats's argument that the goal and value of such poetry is nothing less than "the profane perfection of mankind." An example of Heaney's own exercise of the Herbertian dynamic, the paradoxical and "tension filled" flow that imitates the down-up relationship between gravity and grace, the mundane and the transcendent, can be seen in his important poem titled "Lightenings: viii":

> The annals say: when the monks at Clonmacnoise
> Were all at prayers inside the oratory
> A ship appeared above them in the air.
>
> The anchor dragged along behind so deep
> It hooked itself into the altar rails
> And then, as the big hull rocked to a standstill,
>
> A crewman shinned and grappled down the rope
> And struggled to release it. But in vain.
> "This man can't bear our life here and will drown."
>
> The abbot said, "unless we help him." So
> They did, the freed ship sailed, and the man climbed back
> Out of the marvelous as he had known it. (1998, 338)

Like Herbert's "The Pulley," the poem is built upon an up-down-up rhythm between the transcendent and the ordinary, as well as upon paradox, contradiction, and reversal of expectations. To the crewman from the airborne mystical ship, the ordinary world is both "marvelous" and threatening: "This man can't bear our life here and will drown." The otherworldly crewman may be destroyed by submission to gravity, as indeed a poet can "drown" in the actual. Conversely, the transcendent world of "air" is to him ordinary and safe, yet distinct from the actual world. Heaney's inversion of the conventional views of both "earth" and "air"—and his interpenetrating of these orders of reality in the poem—suggest that both poet and reader must balance both possibilities or "worlds," transcendent and mundane, and live in and move between them. Consciousness and action must inhabit a space in the metaxu yet remain free to negotiate between the two poles. Such rhythm, balance, and tension, as we shall see, are the formal and thematic strategy of the major poems in *The Spirit Level*.

2

THE POET IN THE AGE OF IMBALANCE

Placing Seamus Heaney in relation to the age of imbalance is a daunting challenge. Certainly he shares Simone Weil's critical view of modern Western culture to a considerable degree. Reflecting on the general state of things, he cited with approval Milosz's observation that "no intelligent contemporary is spared the pressure exerted in our world by the void, the absurd, the anti-meaning, all of which are part of the intellectual atmosphere we subsist in" (2002, 49). Heaney's identification with Milosz's view—one shared equally by Weil—is a clue to his own stance toward the age. Milosz, as we saw, argued that the human species is currently undergoing "a great mutation," a shift from the metaphysical to the historical view of man and events, a change that radically alters human consciousness and imagination. Like everyone else, Heaney grew up in and lives in the midst of that "great mutation." To experience this is to experience both self and world as "contradiction," as Weil noted. It is to feel pulled between an intuitive belief in the metaphysical and transcendent hope, on the one hand, and the pulverizing natural and cultural forces that seem to reduce the self to an insignificant cipher swept along on the current of history, on the other. Heaney's struggle and development as a poet has been marked at every stage by this elemental contradiction. Like Weil's principle of metaxu itself, he stands "in between" the contending views—weighing, balancing, judging, and poetically transforming the particular circumstances of his life while trying to hold fast to the root integrity of the personal self.

Like Weil, Milosz, and others, Heaney has pointed to the role of positivism and scientism in the culture's imbalance. Against these forces Heaney argues that poetry must "maintain its centuries-old hostility to reason, science and a science-inspired philosophy" (2002, 356). Positivism's science-inspired ideology cannot account for the mystery of the human predicament, the contradiction of transcendent spirit in the world, or the paradox of gravity and grace. These mysteries are poetry's leverage against the dominant ethos. Heaney registered the negative impact of positivism and scientism in his early poem "Sibyl," a poem as much about modern Western culture as about Ireland:

> My people think money
> And talk weather. Oil-rigs lull their future
> On single acquisitive stems. Silence
> Has shoaled into the trawlers' echo-sounders.
>
> The ground we kept our ear to for so long
> Is flayed or calloused, and its entrails
> Tented by an impious augury.
> Our island is full of comfortless noises." (lines 13–20, 1998, 141)

As the poem reveals, the consumerist ideology of greed, exploitation and profit has come to dominate citizens' consciousness—"My people *think* money"; they are "lulled," "acquisitive," and predatory toward nature's bounty (emphasis added). Milosz noted the spiritual consequences of this debased vision: "The more God abandoned space, the stronger became the dream of building the kingdom of God here and now with our own hands, which, however, condemned man to a life of getting and spending. . . . The pollution of the mind by certain images, those side effects of science, is analogous to the pollution of natural surroundings by technology derived from such science" (2001, 242). Heaney's prognosis in the poem is equally pessimistic. The sibyl, ancient sage, unheard above the din of impious augury, warns that, "unless forgiveness finds its nerve and voice" (line 9, 1998, 141), a regression in our humanity will occur: "I think our very form is bound to change / Dogs in a siege. Saurian relapses. Pismires" (lines 6–7, 1998, 141). Forgiveness demands a change of mind and heart, a *metanoia*, but none is forthcoming in the poem. Yet with typical double consciousness, the speaker personified as the sibyl stands both within and without the culture to judge its dereliction.

With uncanny prescience—"Sibyl" was published as the second section of "Tryptich"—Heaney foresaw the consumerism, the "Celtic Tiger," that would come to dominate Ireland, especially the Republic, from the 1980s to the present. Economic progress, while much needed, brought with it the threat of a regression in humanity, trapping mind and body in the determinism of getting and spending. Viewed from a postmillennium perspective, Heaney's prophetic pessimism seems well founded, since consumerism has nearly replaced sectarian violence as the principal form of gravity in an Irish culture that increasingly mimics the values of mainstream Western society. But like Simone Weil, Heaney pushes against this force of gravity by exposing its possible dire effects upon the human spirit, i.e., its consequences for metaphysical man.

Fully aware of gravity's debilitating force in a culture dominated by positivism and scientism, Heaney is equally conscious of its value as metaxu, i.e., as the necessary ballast or earthboundness that helps define our humanity. Gravity is the in-between-ness or the labyrinth to be negotiated, especially by the poet. Heaney recognized the paradox of gravity and transcendence early in his career, as seen in his poem "Gravities" (1966, 43). The poem explores the tensions between earthbound gravities, the symbols of "home," and various forms of flight—literal, emotional, imaginative. A high-flying kite is reined by "invisible" strings; a flock of pigeons heads toward home; angry lovers reenter "the native port"; and James Joyce, blind in Paris, recalls O'Connell Street and on Iona Comcille once wore "Irish mould next to his feet."

Early in his career the pull of gravity—ties to the familial, religious, and political traditions of the Northern Ireland Catholic community—exercised a dominant influence on Heaney's mind and art. With typical self-scrutinizing candor, he acknowledged this fact in his Nobel Prize address "Crediting Poetry" (1995) when he said that in his early poetry he was too committed to recording actual events in rather documentary fashion and, thus, attending "insufficiently to the diamond absolutes, among which must be counted the sufficiency of that which is absolutely imagined" (1998, 423). Heaney's self-criticism is somewhat overstated, since even early poems like "Digging" reveal something of the "diamond absolutes" in the beauty of their language and form. Nevertheless, his statement does indicate how, at least since the mid-1980s, he has struggled to counterbalance the pull of gravity with more "light" in his poems, more space for "glimpses" of the imagined ideal.

Improved circumstances in Northern Ireland in the 1980s help account for this change in perspective, but it has more to do with his intellectual and poetic development as well as his distancing himself from the immediate conflict. In this regard, Simone Weil can be seen as an important figure in Heaney's struggle to counterbalance the force of gravity and the "diamond absolutes" of the transcendent ideal. In "The Redress of Poetry," he invoked Weil's words and spirit to support his belief that lyric poetry can be a metaphysical, ethical, and political force against the gravitational pull of actual historical events and the zeitgeist of the age. Heaney said that poetry's liberating power can be a force against "the common expectation of solidarity," i.e., the expectation of conformity to the dominant ethos of Western culture and to that of the Northern Ireland community. This expectation of solidarity is rooted in custom, language, inherited cultural rituals, and systems of belief that too often calcify meaning into rigidly prescribed patterns of thought, allegiance, and behavior. Lyric poetry resists such conformity, Heaney claims. It expresses individual consciousness through the beauty of language and form, and it can offer glimpses of an ideal order beyond particular circumstances. Heaney quoted Weil's *Gravity and Grace* to support his argument: "If we know in what way society is unbalanced, we must do what we can to add weight to the lighter side . . . we must have formed a conception of equilibrium and be ever ready to change sides like justice, 'that fugitive from the camp of conquerors.'" He then applied Weil's dictum to lyric poetry:

> "Obedience to the force of gravity. The greatest sin." So Simone Weil wrote in *Gravity and Grace*. Indeed her whole book is informed by the idea of counter-weighing, of balancing out the forces of redress—of tilting the scales of reality toward some transcendent equilibrium. And in the activity of poetry too, there is a tendency to place a counter-reality in the scales—a reality which may only be imagined within the gravitational pull of the actual and can therefore hold its own and balance out against the historical situation. This redressing effect of poetry comes from its being a glimpsed alternative, a revelation of potential that is denied or constantly threatened by circumstances. (1995, 3–4)

Heaney's invoking of *Gravity and Grace* was part of his effort to "show how poetry's existence as a form of art relates to our existence as citizens of society"—how it is "of present use." He wishes to show how "the world of ideal forms also provides the court of appeal through which poetic imagination seeks to redress whatever is wrong or exacerbating in the prevailing conditions" (1995, 1). The phrase "of present use" has a twofold meaning: metaphysical and ethical. First, in an age driven by collectivism and consumerism, poetry can affirm individual man as a unique metaphysical being and not merely a creature entirely subject to history. Second, poetry has ethical power insofar as it resists the dominant culture's forces of gravity. The ethical derives from the metaphysical order, which is based on belief in the transcendent world of "ideal forms" and on what Milosz called "the divine in man." Heaney's citing of Weil in one of his most significant defenses of lyric poetry is important, because he usually cites other poets or literary scholars, and not philosophers, in support of his critical arguments.

Heaney believes that the lyric poem can be "of present use" and still maintain its absolute autonomy as a work of art. In fact, the poem's autonomy is a guarantee of its present use, given the culture's imbalance. Specifically, the lyric poem can be a spiritual force against the age's reductive ethos by widening the "plane of consciousness" to include the transcendent and the numinous and so render justice to the mysterious dimensions of reality. In addition, on the political level it can redress the imbalance by resisting the demand that the poem support—or condemn—a particular political or social agenda. As Heaney observed, such demands "will always want the redress of poetry to be an exercise of leverage on behalf of *their* point of view; they will require the entire weight of the thing to come down on their side of the scales" (2). Heaney himself, of course, has felt such pressure, as section four of "Flight Path" reveals. Riding the train to Belfast, the poet is accosted by an old acquaintance, a militant nationalist, who asks: "When, for fuck's sake, are you going to write something for us?" But the poet stands his ground and replies: "If I do write something, whatever it is, I'll be writing for myself" (1998, 387). Yet Heaney's claim for lyric poetry's ethical force and "present use" should not be construed in any narrow moralistic way, i.e., as to suggest a practical program of action. In one sense poetry changes nothing, as he has acknowledged: "no lyric has ever stopped a tank" (2002, 207). But in a metaphysical sense, it can recall us to our essential humanity by exercising that freedom of mind and imagination that expresses our capacities for grace. We recall that Heaney identifies poetry with the grace of *numen*, that Weil identified grace with "light," and that Milosz spelled out the meaning of that identification: "What, then, is the light? The divine in man turning against the natural in him—in other words, intelligence dissenting from 'meaninglessness,' searching for meaning, grafted onto darkness like a noble shoot onto a wild tree, growing greater and stronger only in and through man"(2001, 238).

For Heaney, the grace of "light" in poetry—the beauty of form, language, and idea—enables the poet to resist ideological bias and to affirm the absolute autonomy of the poem, its free and liberating capacity to "change sides like justice." Changing sides like justice means that the poem can manifest, however obliquely and implicitly, a transcendent scale of truth. Viewed from an aesthetic perspective, what Heaney calls the "fully achieved" poem can counterbalance and "go beyond" the human ethical standard by virtue of its unique mystery, integrity, and beauty as a work of art per se. In its craft and form, the poem can balance and unite ethical and aesthetic truth. Stated differently, the fully achieved poem can balance the ethical gravity of theme, rooted in the actualities of everyday experience, with the grace and mystery of a language and form that suggests the transcendent ideal. Speaking of the free gift of poetry, Heaney said:

> When I say free gift, I mean that lyric poetry, however responsible, always
> has an element of the untrammeled about it. There is a certain jubilation
> and truancy at the heart of an inspiration. There is a sensation of libera-
> tion and abundance which is the antithesis of every hampered and deprived
> condition. And it is for this reason, psychologically, that the lyric poet feels
> the need for justification in a world that is notably hampered and deprived.
> (1989a, xviii)

Liberation through "changing sides like justice" enables the poet to fulfill
William Butler Yeats's famous dictum that the poem "hold in a single thought
reality and justice" (Heaney 2002, 347).

Heaney's attraction to Weil, like that of Milosz, stems from his recognition
that her life and writings demonstrate her "rightness" as an exemplary figure
of the times. As a twentieth-century writer, Weil embodied what Heaney has
called the "solitary role of the witness," the kind of witnessing he finds also
in the work of Wilfred Owen, Osip Mandelstam, Milosz, and Václav Havel
(1995, 4). Each of these writers, while living in extremely difficult personal
circumstances, measured contemporary events against a transcendent ideal and
weighed human injustice on an absolute scale of value. But beyond seeing
Weil as a witness to the transcendent ideal, Heaney equated her concepts of
gravity and grace with "deep structures of thought and feeling derived from
centuries of Christian teaching and from Christ's paradoxical identification
with the plight of the wretched" (3). Heaney is not, I believe, simply referring
to Jesus's empathy with oppressed and marginalized persons.

The point of the statement goes much deeper. Jesus's "paradoxical identification" with the wretched, among which *all* are to be counted, alludes to
the metaphysical union between the divine Son of God and humanity in the Incarnation, the cornerstone of "Christian teaching." In this sense, the wretched
are all those oppressed in body and spirit, i.e., weighed down by the natural forces of gravity. The connection between Jesus and the wretched has
special relevance for the artist. As Katherine Brueck has pointed out, Weil
believed that beauty, truth, and justice are intimately related to human suffering, and all are centered in Jesus's crucifixion. "Any form of beauty . . .
calls attention to the true and the good only insofar as these two qualities
relate to pain. Thus the artist himself must understand human wretchedness
intimately. Only a supreme artistic genius can intone the truth about suffering, i.e., its connection to the good" (Dunaway and Springsted 1996, 110).
Ultimately, Weil viewed human wretchedness as a "function of God's love," the
paradigm for which is Jesus's continuing love for the Father at the moment of his
deepest suffering and abandonment on the cross (110). Jesus's unwavering love

witnesses to the mysterious relationship between truth, justice, and suffering, and of victory masked as apparent defeat, and thus his crucifixion is a liberating act. For Weil, the great artist captures this mystery in his work. Heaney's reference to Jesus and poetry implies that, in its own limited way, lyric poetry can also be such a liberating power. Thus he went on to compare poetry writing to Jesus's writing in the sand when he confronted the accusers ready to stone the adulteress:

> The drawing of those characters is like poetry, a break with the usual life but not an absconding from it. Poetry, like the writing, is arbitrary and marks time in every sense of the phrase. It does not say to the accusing crowd, "Now a solution will take place," it does not propose to be instrumental or effective. Instead, in the riff between what is going to happen and whatever we would wish to happen, poetry holds attention for a space, functions not as distraction but as pure concentration, a focus where our power to concentrate is concentrated back on itself. (1989a, 108)

Poetry is the riff that creates a state of metaxu between the actual "what is going to happen" and the ideal of "what we would wish to happen." In the example Heaney uses here, he suggests that poetry can possibly call to mind an absolute scale of justice, love, and forgiveness that is greater than the woman's accusers' charges. In his paradoxical identification with the plight of the wretched woman and his confrontation with the Law of the accusers, Jesus judges by not judging. His silence and mysterious writing create a space in which his audience, like the reader of poetry, can imagine a view both higher and more humane than that of the judgmental accusers. Since this is possible, then Heaney implies that the poem can counterbalance the narrow perspective of the accusers' tradition-bound legalistic view—equivalent to the community's demand for solidarity—against a wider vision of love and mercy rooted in the ideal. The poem does not explicitly describe such an ideal, but in its power to "hold attention for a space, to concentrate attention back upon itself," it creates a hiatus or interlude that can widen the plane of consciousness into the deeper mystery of the situation.

Heaney describes the kind of liberation of consciousness the poem ideally aims for in *The Government of the Tongue* (1989a):

> The achievement of a poem, after all, is an experience of release. In that liberating moment, when the lyric discovers its buoyant completion and the timeless formal pleasure comes to fullness and exhaustion, something occurs which is equidistant from self-justification and self-obliteration. A plane is—fleetingly—established when the poet is intensified in his being and freed of his predicaments. The tongue, governed so long in the social

> sphere by considerations of tact and fidelity, by nice obeisances to one's
> origins within the minority or the majority, that tongue is suddenly ungov-
> erned. It gains access to a condition this is unconstrained and, while not
> being practically effective, it is not necessarily inefficacious. (xxii)

To achieve such a liberating vision, the poet must negotiate the gravities that
bind him and create an objective voice that both witnesses to the realities of
a reductive age and yet offers, however incipiently, a countervision based on
hope. The effort requires that the poet strive for conscious detachment from
one's emotions in order to develop such an objective voice. Speaking of the
poet's experience of suffering, Heaney cited Carl Jung's insight: "One certainly does feel the affect and is tormented by it, yet at the same time one is
aware of a higher consciousness looking on which prevents one from becoming identified with the affect, a consciousness which regards the affect as an
object, and can say: 'I know that I suffer'" (xxi). As the speaker in "Chekhov on
Sakhalin" says, the writer must "try for the right tone—not tract, not thesis— /
and walk away from floggings" (Heaney 1998, 203).

Heaney's linking of Weil's concepts of gravity and grace, Christian doctrine, and poetry writing reveals the complex and fluid dimensions of his
poetic mind. As his comment about suffering and detachment indicates, he
is a poet both blessed and burdened with double consciousness, a fact that
bears exploring. His invoking Weil and her notions of gravity and grace
reflects his sense of the age's entrapment in dehumanizing antimetaphysical
forces and the need to resist such gravity. Yet many Weil critics, including
Czeslaw Milosz, believe that, despite her claims for the possibility of grace,
her instinctive response to the age was that of a Stoic (2001, 265–66). They
point to her strong emphasis on the deterministic power of Necessity and
the need to submit to it as Jesus did on the cross in her reading of the story
of Christian redemption. They argue that her thought is tilted toward stoic
resignation to gravity, a response that was not surprising given the difficult
circumstances of her life in France before and during World War II. Given
this view of Weil, it is possible to see a kinship between her and Heaney insofar as he shares her pessimistic and, in some degree, stoical response to the
age. Helen Vendler has argued astutely for a strong element of stoicism in his
work, and certainly many of his poems and translations, such as his *Beowulf*,
reveal this element in the seeming fatedness of what happens in the poems. In
this regard, Heaney's secular education and his personal experience, especially
growing up in Northern Ireland in the 1950s and 1960s, reinforced this
stoical element.

On the other hand, critics such as Eric O. Springsted, Tom Werge, and
Katherine T. Brueck emphasize the Christian dimensions of Weil's thought

over the stoical. In particular, Brueck points to the relationship between suffering and divine love manifested in Jesus's crucifixion as the quintessential triumph of grace over necessity. Stoic acceptance is qualified, paradoxically, by inner triumph through outer defeat (Dunaway and Springsted 1996, 112). Heaney would seem to share this view insofar as he affirms the Catholic vision he learned as a youth, i.e., what he called "the visionary possibilities that Catholicism sets alight in the child's mind" (Miller 2000, 36). This vision mitigates the stoical element particularly because it keeps the mind open to possibilities of transformation and transcendence (especially in poetry) in ways that a purely stoical response to experience precludes. In this sense, Heaney seems to follow Milosz more than Weil. But the conflict between the two elements, Stoic and Catholic-Christian, is ongoing in Heaney and is a reflection, I believe, of his double-consciousness as he responds to what he called "the mind's extreme recognitions" (1995, 3).

Heaney's double consciousness can be seen particularly by considering the question of justice, which is a major theme in both his poetry and in Weil's writings. Heaney cited Weil, we recall, when he argued that lyric poetry must resist gravity and the "way society is unbalanced," and to do so the poet "must have formed a conception of equilibrium and be ever ready to change sides like justice, 'that fugitive from the camp of conquerors'" (3). His remark suggests a classical notion of poetic justice of the kind Weil found in Homer's *Iliad*. In her famous essay "The *Iliad*: Poem of Might," she praised Homer's genius in being able to present the Trojan War in a way evenhanded to Greeks and Trojans alike, because he concentrated equally on the *human* tragedy suffered by both sides (Panichas 1977, 153–84; emphasis added). For Weil, Homer's epic reveals how power dehumanizes both victors and vanquished, destroying their souls. War is caused by men abandoning the norm of reason and moderation, the Greek ideal of "measure, of equilibrium which should determine the conduct of life," in favor of overweening ambition for power and domination. Yet once the ideal balance represented by the "golden scales of Zeus" is upset, blind destiny takes its retribution on all involved. Weil says: "because it is blind, destiny establishes a sort of justice, blind also, which punishes men of arms with death by the sword; the *Iliad* formulated the justice of retaliation long before the Gospels, and almost in the same terms" (163). Weil does see evidence of fraternal and familial love, friendship, and hospitality in the *Iliad*, but "such moments of grace are rare" and only seem to sharpen the bitterness wrought by the savagery of war. "Justice and love, for which there can hardly be a place in this picture of extremes and unjust violence, yet shed their light over the whole without ever being discerned otherwise than by accent" (177). We shall see how Heaney treats similar themes in "Mycenae Lookout."

What is especially significant about Weil's view of justice in the essay in relation to Heaney's double consciousness is her claim that the Gospels are an extension of the "Greek genius," a later manifestation of the classical notion of justice:

> [T]his accent (i.e. Greek genius) is inseparable from the idea which inspired the Gospels; for the understanding of human suffering is dependent upon justice, and love is its condition. . . . Greek genius best understood the relation between suffering, justice and love. . . . For the most part the Greeks had such strength of soul as preserved them from self-deception. For this they were recompensed by knowing in all things how to attain the highest degree of lucidity, of purity and simplicity. But the spirit which is transmitted from the *Iliad* to the Gospels, passed on by the philosophers and tragic poets, has hardly gone beyond the limits of Greek civilization. (181)

In the Gospels, of course, Jesus is Weil's model of perfect suffering, justice, and love and of resistance to gravity and power. "Only he who knows the empire of might and knows how not to respect it is capable of love and justice" (181).

In citing Weil in his defense of lyric poetry, Heaney seems to endorse the notion of evenhanded justice and the conception of equilibrium she spelled out in her essay on the *Iliad*. But her conflation of the classical notion of justice and the Gospels is problematic, to say the least, especially if we take seriously Heaney's claim for the importance of his early Catholic training for his poetry. The two views—classical and Christian—are not entirely compatible. Weil has her supporters. For example, Katherine T. Brueck in her fine essay "The Tragic Poetics of Simone Weil" defends Weil's conflation of classical and Christian concepts by focusing on the meaning of human suffering in relation to divine justice in both traditions. In her view, Weil's concentration on unjust suffering, divine love, and justice centered in Jesus's crucifixion is fully compatible with the suffering and justice seen in Homer, Sophocles, and Aeschylus because both represent a supernatural mystery that is logically inexplicable, yet true. "For Weil accursedness is no more separated from justice in Aeschylus and Sophocles or in certain tragedies of Shakespeare and Racine, than it is in the cross of Christ. The link between suffering and justice, however, can only be understood on the level of the supernatural" (Dunaway and Springsted 1996, 115). In Weil's view, only these works (presumably including the gospel narrative) are authentically beautiful. "They direct us to what is true and what is good; they compel us to attend to the mystery of divine love.

This mystery cannot be understood apart from the portrayal of a suffering that is ineradicable. *This is not a suffering which knowledge of a future resurrection may either dissolve or mitigate*" (115; emphasis added).

However, Weil's conflation of Greek thought and the Christian gospel is distorted due to her exclusive focus on Jesus's crucifixion and her disregard of the resurrection. Obsessed with the cross, she brushes aside Jesus's own teaching about his resurrection, and thus she ignores the eschatological meaning of his suffering, death, and resurrection. As F. X. Durrwell has shown, the mystery of Jesus's crucifixion, death, and resurrection must be understood as a single ongoing act that only reaches completion in Christ's glorified body as risen savior (1960, 24–31). This act radically transforms the meaning of history, of the individual person, and of justice. In the Christian view, in contrast to Greek thought, justice concerns justification; that is, the final redemption of mankind from sin and death. Justice in this sense "is only conferred following on the Resurrection" (27). The risen Jesus is God's hand of judgment in history. The Christian view of history is neither cyclical (governed by Fates and destiny) nor stoical. Rather, it is a linear view that affirms movement toward completion in the Parousia and the final triumph of the glorified Christ. Perhaps most importantly, the Greeks could not have known of a crucial vital effect of Jesus's death and resurrection: the coming of the Holy Spirit and its ongoing presence in history. Jesus promised to send the Spirit, an event impossible without Christ's glorification. Under this view, the classical notion of grace is transformed so that now it is the power of the Holy Spirit in the world, in things. Belief in the power of the Holy Spirit is the basis of faith and hope in the here and now.

This Christian vision is the one Heaney would have absorbed in his early Catholic training, and its transfiguring vision persists in his double consciousness along with the Stoic strain, as I have suggested. The impact of the Catholic doctrine of Jesus's incarnation and bodily resurrection on art and aesthetics has been emphasized by George Steiner and William F. Lynch, and their views are apposite any discussion of Heaney's aesthetic. Weil, we recall, said that "earthly things are the criterion of heavenly things" (1970, 137). Steiner linked this idea specifically to the doctrine of transubstantiation in the Eucharist, the sacrament of the real presence of the risen Christ. He then indicated its general significance for art:

> When Shakespeare finds "bodying forth" to imagine the generic presence
> of content within form, he is analogizing directly from (where "to analogize" is also a derivative from the theological) the "real presence" of the
> incarnate in the eucharist. At every significant point, Western philosophies

of art and Western poetics draw their secular idiom from the substratum of Christological debate. Like no other event in our mental history, the postulate of God's *kenosis* through Jesus and from the never-ending availability of the Savior in the wafer and wine of the eucharist, but at a much deeper level, that of our understanding and reception of the truth of art—a truth antithetical to the condemnation of the fictive in Plato. (2001, 67)

For his part, in his seminal study of the literary imagination, *Christ and Apollo* (1960), Lynch described different forms of the imagination and argued that Jesus's incarnation and resurrection changed the metaphysical structure of all created things, the physical world of metaxu as well as human consciousness and imagination, making them potential vehicles of grace. Thus "Christ is water, gold, butter, food, a harp, a dove, the day, a house, merchant, fig, gate, stone, book, wood, light, medicine, oil, bread, arrow, salt, truth, risen sun, way, and many things besides" (183–94).

Steiner and Lynch point to the larger meaning of Heaney's identification of Weil's principles, Jesus's bond with the wretched, and poetry. In the last analysis, the Christian doctrine of the Incarnation forms the theological basis of Heaney's aesthetic, but it is always in tension with the gravity of the stoical element. Nevertheless, it is the basis of his hope, the kind he spoke of when he called witnessing in poetry "an exercise of the virtue of hope." Thus he cited Václav Havel's definition of that hope:

> It is an orientation of the spirit, an orientation of the heart; it transcends the world that is immediately experienced and is anchored somewhere beyond the horizon. I feel that its deepest roots are in the transcendental, just as the roots of human responsibility are. It is not a conviction that things will turn out well, but the certainty that something makes sense, regardless of how it turns out. (1995, 4–5)

Something makes sense "regardless of how it turns out" because hope is not simply a wish for a resolution of difficulties. Rather, it is a theological virtue that finds its "rightness" in the transcendent metaphysical order. It makes sense because it looks to an ideal order of being, a "glimpsed ideal," that may or may not be realized. Havel's definition of hope echoes that of St. Paul: "Now hope that is seen is not hope. For who hopes for what he sees? But if we hope for what we do not see, we wait for it in patience" (Rom 8:24–25). It is also reflected in Heaney's description of the hope vested in Christ in his poem, "Weighing-In"—"the power of power not exercised, of hope inferred / By the powerless forever."

Sustaining a metaphysic of hope in an age antagonistic to transcendent vision is extremely difficult for the poet. Heaney has struggled to affirm that vision and avoid what he called "the quicksand of relativism" and romantic subjectivism, on the one hand, and what I would term the gnosis of rigid stoicism, on the other. The latter especially is a kind of preemptive strike against the mysteries of reality and the dynamics of evolving consciousness. This struggle has shaped his persistent concern with the question of the poet's role in an "unbalanced" culture weighed down by gravity. In the forward to his first collection of essays, *Preoccupations*, he posed the central question of the volume: "What is (the poet's) relationship to be to his own voice, his own place, his literary heritage and his contemporary world?" (1980a, Forward). In response he quoted approvingly Patrick Kavanaugh's remark that in lyric poetry, "the self is only interesting as an example." In a later essay, "Place and Displacement: Recent Poetry from Northern Ireland," Heaney again rehearsed Jung's argument for transcending immediate conflict by developing a higher consciousness to explain how Northern Irish poets "outgrow" their historical situation by transforming subjective voice into what can be called exemplary voice (2002, 122–46). The goal of this development is to overcome the parochialism of adhering to narrowly partisan views—cultural, philosophical, or religious. Inclusive consciousness means freedom of mind and imagination; it means freedom to include the numinous and openness to mystery. The aim is to transform the voice of the subjective self into a witnessing exemplary voice. As Heaney said:

> The poet is stretched between politics and transcendence and is often displaced from a confidence in a single position by his disposition to be affected by all positions, negatively rather than positively. This, and the complexity of the present situation, may go some way toward explaining the large number of poems in which the Northern Irish writer views the world from beyond the grave, from the perspective of mythological or historically remote characters. . . . These poems of the voice from beyond are beamed back out of a condition of silence and Zen-like stillness, an eternity in love with the products of time. (129–31)

This "voice from beyond" is what I have called exemplary voice and is analogous to Weil's decreated ego-self insofar as she called for a detachment from self and its immediate desires. Such detachment would enable the poet to transcend what Heaney called, in reference to Yeats, "the body heat of the pathetic and subjective in art, his embrace of the dramatic and the heroic, his determination to establish the crystalline standards of poetic imagination as normative for the level at which people should live" (353). For Heaney, Yeats admirably fulfilled the poet's task to transform experience into poems that are, metaphysically and ethically, of "present use," because he possessed "a frame of mind which allowed the venturesomeness of a supernatural faith to co-exist with a rigorously skeptical attitude" (348).

However, overcoming subjectivity to achieve exemplary voice does not mean renouncing personal perspective. In this respect Heaney the poet differs from Weil the stoic philosopher. Once again, Milosz pinpointed the problem. In his essay on Lev Shestov, Milosz noted that Weil's view of the "terrifying beauty" of the world was linked to "mathematical Necessity," i.e., the determinism of nature. Though she allowed for the possibility of grace, her thought was shaped by commitment to reason and a "Greek wisdom that led to Stoical resignation." Given that necessity ruled the world, Weil felt that one must embrace its "blind indifference and blind brutality. Only in such a manner does love become impersonal." Shestov and Milosz disagreed, seeing in Weil's view "a glimmer of the old Greek nostalgia for the immutable, eternal, general Oneness in which the particular disappears." But Milosz then asks: "Why should we hate 'I'? Was it not the 'I' of Job that complained and wailed? Was not the God who would demand such an impossible detachment from us a God of the philosophers rather than a God of the prophets?" Milosz argued that Weil's "response to these questions points to her latent Platonism and the Platonic myth of the world as a prison of souls longing after their native land, the empyrean of pure ideas. Many of her maxims amount to a confession of guilt, the basic guilt of existing and to a desire for self-annihilation." He concludes that while Weil recognized that complete renunciation was impossible, she rated the very aspiration as "a high spiritual attainment" (2001, 278–79).

Milosz's criticism of Weil is important for understanding Heaney's notions of exemplary poetic voice for two reasons. First, even though his call for detachment and transcendence of subjectivity mirrors in some degree Weil's decreation, Heaney does not eschew the personal voice or personal imagination. For example, commenting on Patrick Kavanaugh's later poems, on his shift to a lighter, freer voice from the gravity and *gravitas* of his early collection, *The Great Hunger*, Heaney said: "I have come to value this poetry of inner freedom very highly. It is an example of self-conquest, a style discovered to express this poet's unique response to his universal ordinariness, a way of reestablishing the authenticity of personal experience and surviving as an ordinary being" (1989a, 14). (A similar shift can be found in Heaney's voice, of course, beginning with *Seeing Things*.)

The second reason Milosz's criticism of Weil is important for understanding Heaney's poetic voice is a philosophical and theological one. His endorsement of a poetic voice that is "objective" and exemplary is rooted, I believe, in his belief in a metaphysical order of reality. While in this belief his thought resembles Weil's, his endorsement of the personal element in poetic voice is rooted in Christian personalism. Whereas stoicism calls for a self-denial, an erasure of the ego, and passive acceptance of the world of Necessity, Christian personalism affirms the absolute significance of the person and his or her experience. Ultimately this absolute significance derives from the theology of the incarnation, crucifixion, and bodily resurrection of Jesus. The Resurrection, and the continuing presence of the Holy Spirit in the world, affirms the person and makes possible the transfiguration of nature by grace. Weil's rational and stoic inclinations, her dehistoricizing of Jesus into a general model, cannot fully account for such possible transfigurations in the world. Given this, her tilt toward self-renunciation and her negative view of personal imagination is understandable. But Heaney's emphasis on the value of the personal, rooted in his early training, strikes a balance with Weilian stoicism, one that enables him to create a poetic voice that operates "in between" gravity and grace.

The poet whose voice speaks from "in between" gravity and grace is able to write poems that are fully relevant to everyday life and at the same time inspire a hope for greater human fulfillment. As Heaney said:

> We go to poetry, we go to literature in general, to be forwarded within our-selves. The best it can do is give us an experience that is like fore-knowledge of certain things which we already seem to be remembering. What is at work in the most original and illuminating poetry is the mind's capacity to conceive a new plane of regard for itself, a new scope for its own activity. (1995, 159–60)

This goal of rendering full poetic justice to the ideal as well as to the actual world is a hallmark of much of Heaney's mature poetry. At the same time, it is the grounding principle for his artistic detachment from direct involvement in ideological and political squabbles, especially in Northern Ireland, though his poems do have political implications and force. Heaney believes that poetry, by invoking the transcendent ideal, can provide a standard of truth and justice by which to measure the age. Like Weil, Heaney wishes to affirm the truth of an ideal that can, as Weil said, help us "grow wings to overcome gravity," or, as Heaney wrote in "The Gravel Walks," help us to "walk on air against our better judgement." Lyric poetry, he affirms, "can be as potentially redemptive and possibly as illusory as love" (1989a, xxii).

3

THE SPIRIT LEVEL

The title of Heaney's eleventh volume of poetry, *The Spirit Level*, reveals, on one important level, his effort to redress the imbalance of the age, as Weil did, by affirming the capacities of the human spirit to transcend the forces of gravity dominating modern culture. That Heaney would choose this title for the volume indicates the overall thrust of his vision: his concern with the interplay of gravity and grace and the power of art to redress imbalances. The guiding impulse behind the whole collection echoes Weil's insight that "we have to discover the original pact between spirit and the world in the very civilization of which we form a part" (1997, 210). Heaney's volume undertakes such a discovery. The short lyric from which the volume's title is taken, "The Errand," playfully suggests this counterbalancing of the spirit of imagination and actuality. A father tells his son to run

> like the devil
> And tell your mother to try
> To find me a bubble for the spirit level
> And a new knot for this tie.

But the son recognized it as a "fool's errand" and "stood my ground," then waited for "the next move in the game" (1998, 404). The exchange between father and son sets the father's playful imagining against the son's solidly grounded realistic intelligence, the two poles of grace and gravity, which shape the formal and epistemological dynamic of most of the poems in the volume. Like the poet, the son manages to stand his ground in the actual, knowing that the quest for "a bubble" for the spirit level is a frothy "fool's errand." Yet the father's request becomes the avenue for a spiritual bond between father and son, as the latter trumps his father's smile at the joke by recognizing the impossibility of the request. Together, father and son embody dual aspects of vision in "the game," which, like poetry itself, is a matter of weighing and balancing imaginings and hard actualities.

Art's Salvation

The first poem in all of Heaney's collections provides an important clue to the focus of the volume, and *The Spirit Level* is no exception. "The Rain Stick" develops these major themes of gravity, grace, and counterbalancing and in the process illustrates Heaney's subtle application and transformation of Weilian principles. In *Gravity and Grace* (1997), we recall, Weil maintained that "all the *natural* movements of the soul are controlled by laws analogous to those of physical gravity. Grace is the only exception. . . . We must always expect things to happen in conformity with the laws of gravity unless there is supernatural intervention," i.e., a movement of grace (45). As he stated in his interview with Miller, Heaney came to recognize such movements of grace in the affirmations of order, meaning, and beauty expressed in poetry.

On one level "The Rain Stick" is an invocation, a call to readers to direct the soul's attention to the small instrument and hear "a music that you never would have known / To listen for." In an age distracted from the numinous and spiritually out of balance, Heaney asks us to attend to the "music" of an unpretentious instrument that might easily be disregarded, yet which has the power to manifest the basic principle of art's graceful action upon the soul. Alternatively, to turn a deaf ear to the rain stick's value, that is, to ignore the grace and beauty of art, is to submit to the laws of gravity, for Weil "the greatest sin."

As a musical instrument, the rain stick works on the principle of gravity. The speaker/listener, a surrogate for both artist and audience, manipulates the laws of gravity—balance, equilibrium, and flow—to create a music that is "undiminished" and eminently repeatable:

> Up-end the rain stick and what happens next
> Is a music that you never would have known
> To listen for. (1998, 371)

Like any work of art, the poem metaphorically "controls," concentrates, and reshapes natural forces: "Downpour, sluice-rush, spillage and backwash," a trickling gutter, "a sprinkle of drops out of the freshened leaves . . . subtle little wets off grass and daisies . . . glitter-drizzle, almost-breaths of air," even just "the fall of grit." As in so many of Heaney's poems, flowing water, a fluid link between earth and heaven, is his familiar emblem for the movement of the spirit. Here, the speaker's meticulous attention to nature's details reveals a consciousness focused on the metaxu with humble regard and trust in their spiritual efficacy. As in Herbert's "The Pulley," the mystery and beauty of the rain stick and of the poem itself is in the dynamic flow of forces translated into sound and not in static balance or equilibrium.

Yet at the same time, Heaney suggests a transcendent principle of order and balance by the "diminuendo" that "runs through all its scales / Like a gutter stopping trickling." The principle of the musical scale derives from a larger cosmic scale of order, regularity, degree, and relation within the natural order. Again, as we saw, Weil equated the dynamic of music with the descent of grace into the metaxu:

> This movement of descent, the mirror of grace, is the essence of all music. All the rest only serves to enshrine it. The rising of the notes is a purely sensorial rising. The descent is at the same time a sensorial descent and a spiritual rising. Here we have the paradise which every being longs for: where the slope of nature makes us rise to the good. (1997, 206–7)

In "The Rain Stick," the "paradise which every being longs for" is associated with the transforming power of art—the "grace" of vision it offers. Heaney transforms the speaker and the reader metaphorically into a rain stick to emphasize this power: "You stand there like a pipe / Being played by water," so that "You are like a rich man entering heaven / Through the ear of a rain-drop." Heaney revises Jesus's analogy—when he compared the difficulty for a rich man to enter heaven as being like the passage of a camel through "the eye of a needle"—in order to offer a metaphorical salvation through art. The image of entering heaven "through the ear of a raindrop" recalls St. Paul's argument that salvation comes from hearing, as well as Jesus's own words: "Blessed are those who have not seen and yet . . . believe" (John: 20:29).

Here, the "glimpsed ideal" of salvation is linked to the experience of art, both in the making and in the hearing, an experience wherein the gravity of things is imaginatively transformed. As the maker of the rain stick reshaped a simple cactus reed in order to reshape natural sound into "a music," so also the poet reshapes language into art. In its central themes and poetic movement, "The Rain Stick" affirms the central Weilian principle that undergirds all of *The Spirit Level*. As she said, creation "is composed of the descending movement of gravity, the ascending movement of grace and descending movement of the second degree . . . grace is the law of the descending movement" (1997, 48).

Weil argued that gravity's force pulls us away from the transcendent and from God, and that, in the ordinary human condition, we are consigned to its power. As she said: "we must always expect things to happen in conformity with the laws of gravity unless there is supernatural intervention" (45). The natural human condition, then, is one of imbalance and radical limitation, against which "the divine in man" pushes, as Milosz said. From our perspective as ordinary creatures, no "ideal" order is actually possible or approachable without grace. But the ideal can be called to consciousness, made the focus of our attention, and used to measure the actual. Heaney's short lyric "The Poplar" both presents an emblem of this natural "fallen" condition and, as a poem, counters the pull of gravity:

> Wind shakes the big poplar, quicksilvering
> The whole tree in a single sweep.
> What bright scale fell and left this needle quivering?
> What loaded balances have come to grief? (lines 1–4, 1996, 61)

The poem's central analogy between the poplar and the scale points to a fall from an imagined "bright scale" of equilibrious being and justice, the "golden scales of Zeus" that Weil saw as the classical image of cosmic justice (1997, 24–25). The forces of gravity now rule creation; the scale of a transcendent ideal of justice is shattered. Yet while acknowledging the truth of this fallen condition, Heaney redresses the situation poetically because the poem itself, a tight, neatly balanced quatrain, creates an order and beauty that counterbalances the poem's argument. The lovely "quicksilvering" (i.e., etymologically, "living" and mercurial) of the leaves imaginatively transforms the poplar in the speaker's vision into a "needle quivering," so that the natural beauty of the tree's shimmering light (grace) becomes a bright reminder of the ideal. Yet Heaney does not insist. Instead, he poses the analogy between the actual tree and the transcendent "bright scale" as a metaphysical question in a world that has "come to grief," leaving us with a glimpsed cosmic mystery to be pondered.

The poem's beauty recalls Weil's lucent observation: "Beauty is the providential dispensation by which truth and justice, while still unrecognized, call silently for our *attention*" (1977, xxxi). The speaker's relation to the poplar underscores the need for such attention, because it recalls us to our true condition as creatures linked to the transcendent. For Weil, attention "consists of suspending our thought, leaving it detached, empty, ready to be penetrated by the object; it means holding in our minds, within reach of this thought . . . the diverse knowledge we have acquired which we are forced to make use of." The state of attention is chiefly characterized by "waiting" for true insight;

ultimately, waiting for God (1977, 49–50). Weil's concepts of attention and waiting are echoed in Heaney's view of poetry as a "riff," a concentration of consciousness back upon itself, of waiting and "marking time," as he noted when he compared the "riff" of poetry to the suspension of time when Jesus wrote in the sand. The poplar tree/fallen scale analogy beautifully focuses our attention on the enlarged and enlarging vision of the transcendent reality represented metaphorically through the lovely tree.

Two Sides—Weight and Balance

The harsh fact of gravity's power in a world absent any "bright scale" points to the central theme of justice and injustice in both *Gravity and Grace* and *The Spirit Level*. Imagined ideal notwithstanding, gravity rules the actual world. In Heaney's "Mycenae Lookout," as we shall see, the watchman says he stands "ready made" to serve a god of justice if he would come down from heaven, but no god of justice appears. For her part, Weil defined justice as "the exercise of supernatural love," and in her "Forms of the Implicit Love of God," she noted that "the even balance, an image of equal relations of strength, was the symbol of justice from all antiquity" (1951, 146). Yet the ordinary world suffers under the imbalance of injustice. Heaney's complex parable of moral ambiguity and Weilian contradiction, "Weighing In," makes this clear. Its title evokes both a natural weigh scale and, remotely, the absolute scale of justice analogized in "The Poplar." More ominously, it suggests a pugilistic weighing in for combat, an exercise of force and raw power. Noting this pugilistic theme, Daniel Tobin, in his excellent study of Heaney's poetry, has argued that the poem challenges the orthodox Christian ideal of altruistic love (1999, 285). Yet when viewed from a complex Weilian perspective, i.e., in terms of her belief in existential contradiction, the poem seems to subvert that challenge to Christian orthodoxy as well, leaving its moral paradoxes, as in Herbert's "The Pulley," unresolved and open to further ponderings. The poem not only subverts orthodoxy, in my view, but also dramatizes the insoluble moral dilemmas of living in the metaxu, and in so doing it creates a mystery that subverts both the orthodox Christian ideal and the challenge to it. As a result, the poem becomes an agonizing dialogue of self and soul over the speaker's relationship with another human being, as well as a paradigm of all conflicted relationships burdened by the weight of gravity. As is typical, Heaney creates an open-ended "ending," leaving the reader to reflect upon the mystery. The "just balance" hinted at in the titular scale image is never realized.

Heaney's opening image in the poem, the "56 lbs. weight," a "solid, iron / Unit of negation," is a natural metaphor for the force of gravity. "Gravity's black box," the speaker calls it, "a *life-belittling* force" (emphasis added). Still, he says, it can be counterbalanced on a weigh-bridge, so that "everything trembled, flowed with give and take." But such physical equilibrium is rarely attainable in the human moral realm, where issues of judgment, egotism, power, personal integrity, honor, and revenge become inextricably interwoven. Christian charity commands forbearance and self-denial in the face of wrong, the speaker says. It is what,

> good tidings amount to:
> This principle of bearing, bearing up
> And bearing out, just having to
>
> Balance the intolerable in others
> Against our own, having to abide
> Whatever we settled for and settled into
>
> Against our better judgment. Passive
> Suffering makes the world go round. (lines 13–21, 1998, 382)[10]

In this section, the speaker seems to prescribe Weilian self-denial and decreation as a moral stance. For her, passive suffering is "the only way of salvation"; it "is the work of grace and not of the will" (1997, 23–24). One is called to renounce willful action in favor of resignation to necessity and, with love and complete attention to the divine being, to wait for grace to descend. The goal of decreation is to subvert the egoistic self and personal desire, and, as always for her, Christ is the ideal example of this posture.

Such a posture certainly affirms a moral ideal, but Heaney's revision of the conventional cliché—"Love makes the world go round"—suggests that the dictum is too simplistic an answer for the inner spiritual conflict represented in the poem. As the speaker says, the principle

> holds good only as long as the balance holds
> The scales ride steady and the angels' strain
> Prolongs itself at an unearthly pitch.

Weil's Christian ideal exists, but Heaney's puns on "strain" and "unearthly" underscore the near impossibility of realizing this superhuman ideal in the ordinary human world. Moreover, when forbearance becomes a mask for cowardice or conformity, for doing "the decent thing" at the expense of individual human spirit, it is "against our better judgment" and a "life-belittling force." But lest we oversimplify this laudable viewpoint, Heaney's use of the phrase "against our better judgement" is ambiguous. In "The Gravel Walks," as we shall see later, he uses the phrase positively to suggest the need to transcend the gravity of reason and "good judgement" by reaching for the ideal—"So walk on air against your better judgement." The effect of the ambiguity here creates a "loaded" balance of opposites—ideal action vs. human weakness—deepening the moral complexities developed in the poem. For the speaker the conflict between noble ideal and personal desire becomes acute. As Thibon noted, even for Weil "nothing is more degrading than a noble action performed in an unworthy spirit" (Weil, 1997, 24). We recall that in "Station Island" the ghost of James Joyce cautions the outsetting poet against passive subservience to "doing the decent thing," because it risks undermining individual spirit, voice, and freedom (Heaney 1998, 245).

Section two of the poem further complicates Weil's ideal of Christian forbearance as the speaker questions his first noble statement:

To refuse the other cheek. To cast the stone.
Not to do so some time, not to break with
The obedient one you hurt yourself into

Is to fail the hurt, the self, the ingrown rule. (lines 25–28, 1998, 383)

When forbearance becomes an "ingrown rule," so that it is virtually an unconscious response, personal freedom is stifled. Paradoxically, rigid or unconscious adherence to the rule devalues both the sufferer, the principle of forbearance, and justice itself. It is perhaps significant to note, in this respect, Heaney's editing of Weil's dictum ("Obedience to the force of gravity. The greatest sin.") when he cited it in "The Redress of Poetry." Weil's remark comes from a passage in *Gravity and Grace* (1997) that speaks directly to the situation in this poem. She admitted that when she suffered intense migraine headaches she wanted to "make another being suffer" by hitting him on the head. Then she added: "When in that state, I have several times succumbed to the temptation at least to say words which cause pain. Obedience to the force of gravity. The greatest sin" (47). Weil chastised herself for succumbing to natural impulse and for causing pain. In "Weighing In," however, the speaker weighs the value of passive forbearance and passivity against the impulse to strike out against another and does resist the impulse. Nevertheless, he views his forbearance as ignoble, cowardly, and "life-belittling."

Weil called obedience "the supreme virtue" and "the only pure motive." But she distinguished between two kinds of obedience:

We can obey the force of gravity or we can obey the relationship of things. In the first case we do what we are driven to by the imagination which fills up empty spaces. . . . If we suspend the filling up activity and fix our attention on the relationship of things, a necessity becomes apparent which we cannot help but obey. . . . The obedience must, however, be obedience to necessity and not to force (terrible void in the case of slaves). (90–98, passim)

Obedience to necessity and focusing on "the relationship of things" demands self-effacing decreation, because the relationship is ultimately rooted in a right relationship to God, who is supernatural love. Thus Weil said: "In contemplation, the right relationship with God is love, in action it is slavery. This distinction must be kept. We must act as becomes a slave while contemplating with love."[11]

Weil's model for obedience to necessity and for perfect forbearance is, of course, Jesus, the obedient Son who took the form of a slave out of love for mankind. But in "Weighing In," Heaney's speaker questions, though without completely denying, the value of Jesus's passive obedience:

> *Prophesy who struck thee!* When soldiers mocked
> Blindfolded Jesus and he didn't strike back
>
> They were neither shamed nor edified, although
> Something was made manifest—the power
> Of power not exercised, of hope inferred
>
> By the powerless forever. (lines 31–36, 1998, 383)

Here, Jesus's divine power goes unexercised; instead, the power of divine love was "made manifest." Christ is obedient to God the Father's will ("Not what I want but what you want" [Matthew 26:39]). As the previous quotation shows, Heaney balances the immediate human ineffectualness of Jesus's passivity against the invisible power of a transcendent principle of love and hope that is paradoxically perfected in weakness—"hope inferred // By the powerless forever." Yet while he credits the power of the Christian ideal of perfect forbearance and kenosis modeled in Jesus, the speaker also recognizes the human failure to live up to it and the natural impulse to revolt against "the ingrown rule."

> Still, for Jesus' sake,
> Do me a favor, would you, just this once?
> Prophesy, give scandal, cast the stone.

Like the second thief crucified with Jesus, the speaker wants to see a refusal to submit to gravity and an exercise of divine power. But of course such actions would destroy the paradox of Jesus's redemption of mankind through submission to the divine will and undermine the Christian belief that the ultimate realization of the human spirit—of body and soul—is only possible because of Jesus's self-emptying death on the cross and bodily resurrection.

To her credit, Weil also recognized the same dilemma of action versus forbearance and the sheer human difficulty of rising to the ideal. She said: "Judge not. Christ himself does not judge. He is our judge. Suffering innocence is the measure. . . . Not to judge. This is not indifference or abstraction; it is transcendent judgment, the imitation of divine judgment *which is not possible for us*" (1997, 190; emphasis added). The ordinary human impulse is to judge, to strike back, to try to answer the perceived wrong or injustice. Weil said: "To forgive. We cannot do this. When we are harmed by someone, reactions are set up within us. The desire for vengeance is a desire for essential equilibrium; . . . it is impossible to forgive whoever has done us harm if that harm has lowered us" (50–51).

In "The Redress of Poetry" Heaney said that the poet, ideally, must be able to "change sides like justice, that 'fugitive from the camp of conquerors.'" "Weighing In" employs that poetic principle with its back-and-forth flow of ethical arguments, the weighing of responsibility, and the possible alternatives of action the speaker broods over. Like Heaney's earlier "Exposure" and "Punishment," this poem can also be seen to represent the poet's uneasy agonizing over his "responsible *tristia*," the conflict between ideal ethical principles (and poetry's absolute value), on the one hand, and the call for immediate and direct political action, on the other. Such dilemmas, as well as intimations of the "glimpsed ideal," can be dramatized in a poem, but they are almost impossible to resolve in the actual world. Nevertheless, Heaney's grappling with such complex issues in "Weighing In" is another demonstration of how poems can be "of present use."

Like Herbert, Heaney registers this value through paradox and irony, especially in the last section of the poem. The speaker admits that there are "Two sides to every question, yes, yes, yes," but still chastises himself for "not just weighing in . . . without any self-exculpation or self-pity. . . . I held back when I should have drawn blood // And that way (*mea culpa*) lost an edge." He does not strike back. But his obedience to "the ingrown rule," he feels, was cowardice rather than virtue, "a deep mistaken chivalry." As he realizes, the ingrown rule has itself become a weight of gravity he could not break free of so as to be true to the "better judgment" of his inner self. Earlier, we saw how Heaney affirmed Jung's thesis about the need to resolve insoluble conflict by developing a "new level of consciousness" to create greater self-awareness, detachment from emotion, freedom, and transcendence. But here the speaker only chides himself for not using force. He neither strikes to avenge the wrong nor chooses to forgive. For her part, Weil saw brute force as the operative principle in the twentieth century, and she vigorously condemned it: "supernatural love (i.e. true justice) has no contact with force" (1997, 23). But the speaker in "Weighing In" achieves neither a full Jungian transcendence of conflict nor Weil's spiritual renuncia- tion of force, though the poet seems to achieve some liberation by objectify- ing the conflict in the poem. The speaker is still trapped in impotency and self-recrimination. However, Heaney further compounds these moral para- doxes when we recall—as the poet surely does—that Jesus himself on many occasions opposed following the "ingrown rule" when it is done merely for civility's sake, that is, out of conformity to social norm by doing what in the eyes of the world is considered "the decent thing."

"Weighing In" does credit Jesus as an exemplary model whose inner spiritual power and freedom were perfected in defeat and death. But the speaker is not Jesus. He is caught in the world of gravities—the "56 lbs. weight"—neither perfectly obedient nor free, a truth admitted ruefully in the last line: "At this stage only foul play cleans the slate." Ironically, for Weil even such desire to "clean the slate" and balance the wrong is misguided. "The search for equilibrium is bad because it is imaginary. Even if in fact we kill or torture our enemy it is, in a sense, imaginary" (51). Heaney's poem is thus a weighing of moral and artistic conscience, one that refuses any easy resolution of the dilemmas it dramatizes. But what resolution is possible? The answer, for Weil, would be an act of forgiveness and love and the freedom such action would bring. For her, we recall, love of neighbor is one of the supreme manifestations of God's presence in the world. Heaney affirms such an insight in his tribute to poet Hugh MacDiarmid, "An Invocation." In that poem the speaker asks: "Who is my neighbor?" and answers: "My neighbor is all mankind." But such an insight is not forthcoming in "Weighing In." Instead, what we witness in the poem is an internalizing of the metaxu in the speaker. His mind itself becomes a kind of psychological weigh-bridge for the struggle between the ideal and the actual, each given its due weight in a manner that vivifies the inescapable ambiguities of consciousness and conscience. At the same time, however, we can say that the poem's very open-endedness "furthers" consciousness insofar as it deepens awareness of the moral nuances of the conflict without settling for any easy resolution, either orthodox or heterodox.

Significantly, there are no images of light in "Weighing In." Instead, Heaney emphasizes the gravitational forces that trap the speaker in egotism, passion, self-doubt, and frustrated revenge. Yet these human failings are explicitly measured against the absolute standard of love, self-denial, and divine justice personified in Jesus's suffering and crucifixion. Jesus on the cross, as we saw, is always Weil's model of perfect justice, which she equated with supernatural love. "The Passion is the existence of perfect justice without any admixture of appearance. Justice is essentially non-active. It must be either transcendent or suffering. The Passion is purely supernatural justice, absolutely stripped of all sensible help, even of the love of God insofar as it can be felt" (1997, 143). For Weil, Jesus's incarnation and death is the axis point of "balance" between the divine and human world, between the gravity of an always-imbalanced world and supernatural grace. The cross is the weigh-bridge of all creation.

Treadmill and Waterwheel

The ideal of perfect justice and love Weil saw personified in Jesus on the cross and the vision of hope it represents is even more remote in Heaney's brilliant meditation on human power, force, and violence, "Mycenae Lookout." The scene in the poem is Argos at the moment of Agamemnon's return from the Trojan War, but given the poem's imagined moral range, it might well be Beirut, Rwanda, Bosnia, Palestine, Belfast, Baghdad, or any other scene of twentieth-century brutality and murder. On one level "Mycenae Lookout" records Heaney's angry reaction at the time to the stalled peace negotiations and the ongoing sectarian violence in Northern Ireland in the 1990s. Troy and Argos stand as images of a violent civilization spiraling toward destruction. Yet the real subject of the poem, like that of Weil's famous essay, "The *Iliad*: Poem of Might," is the brutal exercise of power throughout history, the gravity of force seen in the cyclic violence within the human family that leaves everyone a victim, with "no innocent bystanders." As Weil said of war, its "power to transform man into a thing is double and it cuts both ways: it petrifies differently but equally the souls of those who suffer it, and of those who wield it" (Panichas 1977, 173). Gravity governs this brutal world, and any imagined ideal of justice—human or divine—is largely absent from the actual events at Troy and Argos. For Greek and Trojan alike, violence becomes a self-perpetuating principle of power, as Weil echoes Thucydides' view of the inexorable law of necessity governing relations between powerful rivals (Nevin 1991, 130). In Heaney's poem, the violence is primordial, sexual, and atavistic as he revisits and deepens the theme of brutal power registered in his earlier volume, *North*. The clamor of war and lust, the erotics of violence—of

military, political, and sexual power—seem to drown out the human voice
("The ox is on my tongue"), except for the bleating cries of the victims and
the agonized voice of the witness.

The speaker in "Mycenae Lookout" is the watchman in Agamemnon's
house, but of course he is also a figure of the poet. In this dual role, he per-
sonifies the writer as witness that Heaney so admires in Mandelstam, Milosz,
Owen, Weil, and others. As a servant of the royal household he is powerless.
But in his role as truth-speaking poet-witness, he serves as a countervoice
to the deception and brutality unfolding in Argos. Because he stands partly
outside the bloodbath and partly complicit in it, in his *agon* the watchman
identifies with the plight of the suffering, as Heaney says the poet must.
In addition, as a poet-witness, he exemplifies Weil's principle of resistance
to gravity, as well as Heaney's notion of the poet who explore the mind's
"extreme recognitions" of both the facts and possible alternatives of action
(1995, 3). Such witnessing in voice and vision on behalf of humanity is,
for Heaney, one way poetry can be of "present use" by truthfully recording
what happened. In "Weighing In," as we saw, the speaker tried unsuccess-
fully to balance the claims of justice, power, passive suffering, and the desire
for revenge, but without success. He remained locked in the vicious cycle of
gravity. Paralyzed, he could neither follow the Christian ideal of forgiveness
nor act without self-recrimination and guilt. Though the context here is classical rather than Christian, the watchman faces a similar but far more complicated moral dilemma. Like the speaker in "Weighing In" (and in the
earlier "Punishment"), he weighs his "responsible *tristia*" but is unable to act
decisively. His burden is compounded by his lowly position as a servant in
Agamemnon's house. His mind is wracked by his "honour-bound" allegiance
to King Agamemnon, his knowledge of Clytemnestra's adultery with Aegisthus, his prophetic foreboding and foreknowledge of the disaster to come,
and his awareness that his failure to warn the king will allow the queen's
plan of revenge to unfold. Appeal to the gods, to divine justice, seems a
futile gesture in this blood-soaked world. As throughout much of history,
gravity and fate rule the stage. And so, in a futile appeal to the heavens, the
watchman laments:

> If a god of justice had reached down from heaven
> For a strong beam to hang his scale-pans on
> He would have found me tensed and ready-made.
> I balanced between destiny and dread
> And saw it coming, clouds bloodshot with the red
> Of victory fires, the raw wound of that dawn

Igniting and erupting, bearing down
Like lava on a fleeing population. (lines 34–41, 1998, 388)

But no god of justice appears. Zeus' "golden scale" is absent, replaced by the watchman's wavering "balance" between destiny and dread. In the opening section of the poem, the watchman's mind, like the poet's, is strained between contending visions and experiences—Heaney's "extreme recognitions"—that leave him lacerated and suffering. The first is the nightmare vision of "blood in bright webs in a ford," of "bodies raining down like tattered meat," and of cattle being unloaded for slaughter off the "dropped gangplank of a cattle truck"—images of past and present realities, ancient and modern, that fuse in the speaker's nightmare. Thus the torchlight heralding Agamemnon's return becomes "a victory beacon in an abattoir," an image, from Tacitus, of the universal nightmare of history that Heaney spoke of in his Nobel Prize address when he said: "It is difficult at times to repress the thought that history is about as instructive as an abattoir; that Tacitus was right and that peace is merely the desolation left behind after the decisive operations of merciless power" (1998, 422). In contrast, the watchman's second recollection is the bucolic memory of awakening.

when the mist would start
To lift off fields and inlets, when morning light
Would open like the grain of light being split,
Day in, day out, I'd come alive again,
Silent and sunned as an esker on a plain. (line 25–29, 387)

The coming of light, an image of grace that suggests the first dawn of creation, is ironic here, given the horrors about to unfold in Argos when Agamemnon returns. But it is also a harbinger of hope, a recollection of nature's steadfast beauty that anticipates the dawning vision of peace, if only as an interlude between wars, in the final section of the poem.

Because of his inferior position, his divided loyalties, and fearful reluctance to act, the watchman cannot or will not attempt to reverse the course of events in Argos. But as a witness and judge, he can still voice personal judgment on the bloody events, a truth-telling that is important in itself. Therefore he is like the poet, identifying with the universal victims of brutality yet also as a citizen complicit in what happens. In section 2, he witnesses the fate of the unheeded prophetess Cassandra, her very "muteness" and passivity a reproach and a goad to the voluble watchman-poet figure. Cassandra represents all the innocent victims of war, those destroyed willy-nilly by the forces of gravity, injustice, and violence, particularly women subjected to male brutality and sexual exploitation, as in the earlier "Punishment." Heaney's terse triplets underscore how her prophetic wisdom is "clipped" and muted,

> saying, "A wipe
> of the sponge,
> that's it.
>
> The shadow-hinge
> swings unpredictably
> and the light's
>
> blanked out." (lines 103–7, 390)

At least since *North* Heaney has emphasized the link between primal sexual energy and violence throughout history. As Weil said: "War and Eros are the two sources of illusion and falsehood among men. Their mixture represents the very greatest impurity" (1997, 137). Such an atavistic mixture pervades "Mycenae Lookout." Helen and Paris's lust ostensibly initiated the war. But the poison—the corruption of love into lust for power and dominance—is systemic. Heaney equates eros and war when the watchman hears

> The agony of Clytemnestra's love-shout
> That rose through the palace like the yell of troops
> Hurled by King Agamemnon from the ships.

Unchecked, the primal urge contaminates the whole community, and there is

> No such thing
> As innocent
> bystanding.
>
> Though the Argives
>
> could feel
> a missed
> trueness in them
> focus

—a lost vulnerability and innocence—at the sight of ravaged Cassandra, her suffering only provokes

> the resultant
>
> shock desire
> in bystanders
> to do it to her
>
> there and then.

Horribly, the sight of the suffering victim *inspires* erotic desire, not pity. Like Iphigenia before her, Cassandra is led to sacrificial slaughter like "a lamb / at lambing time."

As for any notion of transcendent order, the force of the "gene hammer" of sexual violence and war rules the supernatural as well as the human world in the poem. The sexual escapades and murderous violence of Agamemnon, Clytemnestra, and Aegisthus mirror the action on Mount Olympus,

> where the gods
> and goddesses took lovers
> and made out endlessly.

Any possibility of redeeming grace seems foreclosed in the watchman's nightmare vision of history. Heaney extends the vision of eros and violence down through history when, in the midst of a seemingly pastoral scene, the watchman "sees" Romulus's fratricidal murder of Remus:

> I saw cities of grass,
> Valleys of longing, tombs, a windswept brightness,
> And far off, in a hilly, ominous place
>
> Small crowds of people watching as a man
> Jumped a fresh earth-wall and another ran
> Amorously, it seemed, to strike him down. (lines 128–33, 391)

Though burdened by the weight of events and his own complicity in them, the watchman also reads the deeper meanings in the situation. Like the witness-poet, he stands outside the "claque" of "mouth athletes," the politicians who talk incessantly while the "war stalled in the pre-articulate," the subconscious cauldron of blind passion, betrayal, and revenge. Yet, as a servant, he is frozen into a "cross-purposed silence" and duplicity. He is

> all smiles
> to Aegisthus every morning,
> much favored and self-loathing.

The weight of the "ox's tons of dumb / inertia" stops him from warning Agamemnon, opening the way to another round of fated tragedy:

> My own mind was a bull-pen
> where horned King Agamemnon
> had stamped his weight in gold.
> But when the hills broke into flame
> And the queen wailed on and came,
> it was the king I sold.

. . . this ladder of our own that ran
deep into a well-shaft being sunk
in broad daylight, men puddling at the source

through tawny mud, then coming back up
deeper in themselves for having been there,
like discharged soldiers testing safe ground. (lines 219–24, 394)

The hope for peace and renewal of the community is in the hands and hearts
of these

finders, keepers, seers of fresh water
in the bountiful round mouths of iron pumps
and gushing taps.

The dynamic downward-upward movement of the final section and the
transformation of the "ladder of assault" into the ladder used to find water
metaphorically recapitulates the metaphysical and aesthetic dynamic prescribed by Heaney and Weil. We recall that she saw the double movement
of descent in a work of art as "the mirror of grace . . . to do again, out of
love, what gravity does: Is not the double movement of descent the key to
all art?" (1997, 206). Similarly, we recall Heaney's praise of the up-down-up
dynamic in Herbert's poetry, the fluidity of his artistic and religious impulses,
the grace of his wit counterbalancing the "gravity of his judging and knowing" (1995, 10). The ending of "Mycenae Lookout," with its modulating up-
down-up rhythm and its softened diction ("puddling," "tawny," "bountiful")
dramatizes the same interplay of the forces of gravity and grace, actual and
ideal. Moreover, the "finders, keepers, seers of fresh water" work in "broad
daylight" and emerge "deeper in themselves," suggesting they have located the
"missed trueness" of self-knowledge that the lascivious bystanders who ogled
Cassandra had lost. They have found the source of their truest selves in this
beneficent communal activity.

But what justifies this hopeful movement in the final section of the poem?
What absolves it from the criticism that it is merely a romantic and nostalgic
fantasy arbitrarily imposed to save the poem from grim determinism? For one,
Heaney imagines the hope realistically as rooted in ordinary communal experience; it is a "reminder and a signpost" of a possible return to the humane
spirit that sustains and nourishes our best impulses. Because of this, it is true
to the metaxu, since the hope is centered in actual experience. As such, it
both recalls a peaceful past in the ordinary life outside war and anticipates
a potentially bountiful future. Here, the cycle of the poem moves beyond
violence. The watchman's reverie, unlike his earlier nightmare, turns memory

into hope for deliverance from the vicious cycles of bloodshed. As Weil said, in typically paradoxical fashion:

> The past: something real but absolutely beyond reach, toward which we cannot take one step, toward which we can but turn ourselves so that an emanation of it may come to us. Thus it is the most perfect image of eternal, supernatural reality. (1997, 229)

Perhaps more important, the final section of the poem captures the movement of "nostalgia" that J. M. Baker Jr. explained as the central metaphysical idea in Weil's doctrine of the metaxu. For her, as we recall, nostalgia is not simply a feeling or mood. Rather, it denotes the *structural* relationship of being between the actual and the ideal in the metaxu, which accounts for the inherent "contradiction" in all things. All material things possess their own actual reality yet point to an ideal metaphysical reality. This paradox accounts for the "longing" inherent in all things and our nostalgia for the higher source of spiritual reality beyond the physical. The final section of the poem beautifully and realistically evokes this "moment of nostalgia" for the source, a source that Weil identified ultimately with supernatural love and specifically manifested in love of neighbor.

Moreover, the optimism and hope in the final movement of the poem situates the theme of justice within a higher perspective. The watchman's earlier hope for a "god of justice" to descend fails, and the cycle of bloody revenge unfolds. But for Weil, as we saw, there is a higher unwritten law beyond conventional justice, to which the only response is love. For her, love and ultimate justice are inextricably bound together, as manifested in the paradoxical commands of Christ to forgive and show mercy (Nevin 1991, 350). Again, it is the difference between the Pharisees who demand that the adulteress be punished according to the law and Jesus's forgiving love that transcends their conventional justice. Or in the classical context, it is the difference between Creon and Antigone when Antigone appeals to a higher divine law against Creon's legalism and then defies him in order to bury her brother. The final movement in "Mycenae Lookout," with its images of peace and replenishment—"daylight," "water," "source," "discharged soldiers," "finders, keepers, seers," and "pumps" with "bountiful round mouths"—intimates a norm of peace and fellowship, a world in which the higher law of love and community might possibly be realized. Nostalgia might then become prophesy, the true past reclaimed for the future. Without sentimentalizing, Heaney offers a vision of how the gravity of history's brutalities—ancient and modern—might be redressed. But the choice of "treadmill" or "waterwheel" is left to the reader and to society at large.

Imagining St. Kevin

Imagined ideal notwithstanding, neither the watchman in "Mycenae Look-out" nor the speaker in "Weighing In" can transcend the personal anguish and moral dilemmas caused by their complicity, guilt, and moral paralysis. Neither poem witnesses strongly to the force of a transfiguring love, self-sacrifice, decreation, and obedience to God that Weil saw represented ideally in the person of Jesus. One who does seem to follow the path of Christ is the legendary St. Kevin in "St. Kevin and the Blackbird." Kneeling in his monastic cell with one arm stretched out the window "stiff / As a crossbeam," the saint is "moved to pity" when a blackbird nests in his palm, and so he stays kneeling for weeks until the young are "fledged and flown" (1998, 384). Kevin is a model of Weil's decreated self, one whose self-emptying love for the humble fledglings is a counterweight to earth's gravity. His crossbeam stance, of course, imitates Jesus on Golgotha. As Weil said: "The cross as a balance and as a lever. A going down, the condition of a rising up. Heaven coming down to earth raises earth to heaven;" the "point of leverage is the cross. There can be no other. It has to be at the intersection of the world and that which is not the world. The cross is this intersection" (1997, 145–46). Thibon explained Weil's complex notion of the relation between decreation, passive suffering, the void, and the "third dimension," i.e., supernatural love:

> This process of "decreation," which is the only way of salvation, is the work of grace and not of the will. Man does not pull himself up to heaven by his hair. The will is only useful for servile tasks; it controls the right use of natural virtues, which are prerequisites of the work of grace . . . the divine seed comes from elsewhere. . . . Weil, like Plato and Malebranche, considers attention to be of far more importance than the will. [Decreation enables one to arrive] through self-effacement and love at that state of perfect docility to grace where goodness spontaneously emanates. "Action is the pointer which shows the balance. We must not touch the pointer but the balance." (24)

As Thibon explained further, for Weil, Jesus the passive suffering servant is the perfect model of such attention and decreation:

> Here below God is the feeblest and most destitute of beings; his love, unlike that of idols, does not fill the carnal part of the soul; to go to him we have to labor in the void, to refuse every intoxication of passion or pride which veils the horrible mystery of death, and to allow ourselves to be guided only by the "still, small voice" spoken of in the Bible—a voice inaudible to the senses and unnoticed by the self. . . . Supernatural love has no contact with force. . . . Therefore "the saint is naked" because armor "prevents any direct

contact with reality and above all makes it impossible to enter the third dimension which is that of supernatural love." (22–24, passim)

Heaney's St. Kevin performs this *imitatio Christi* by his compassionate care of the fledgling blackbird. Viewed from a rational, pragmatic, human perspective, his sacrifice may seem foolish, but "divine foolishness" nonetheless, based on love. His cruciform posture makes an intersection between this world and the transcendent, as he finds "himself linked / Into the network of eternal life." Kevin himself is a bridge, a metaxu, linked to earth, bird, and to transcendent eternity. The saint seems to enter the void created by his self-emptying of ego, for Weil the necessary prelude to grace. "Grace fills empty spaces but it can only enter where there is a void to receive it, and it is grace itself which makes this void" (55). Given his posture and his link to the "network of eternal life," Kevin has apparently entered the grace-filled state Weil called "the third dimension" of supernatural love.

But notwithstanding the saint's beatific gesture, Heaney's complex perspective in the poem raises more probing questions than any orthodox or even heterodox theological reading can easily circumscribe. Contra Weil's mystical view, the self-conscious speaker in the poem poses a series of questions that attempt to discover the inner meaning of Kevin's actions. If we examine the voice of the speaker, we see that Heaney has counterbalanced saint and speaker, and the interaction of the two perspectives becomes the real dynamic fulcrum of meaning in the poem, its intellectual and artistic crossbeam. For example, after describing the saint's posture, the speaker opens the second section of the poem with a series of questions:

> And since the whole thing's imagined anyhow,
> Imagine being Kevin. Which is he?
> Self-forgetful or in agony all the time
>
> From the neck on out down through his hurting forearms?
> Are his fingers sleeping? Does he still feel his knees?
> Or has the shut-eyed blank of underearth
>
> Crept up through him? Is there distance in his head? (lines 13–19, 1998, 384)

The questions themselves are ambiguous. Is he "self-forgetful" because of his link to the eternal? Or is he "in agony" because he is *consciously* suffering, or is he so oblivious as to not feel anything? Does he feel pain, what for Weil is the necessary path through the void to transcendence, or is he numb (fingers, knees) and beyond feeling? Has he transcended the world and entered a mystical state, the "third dimension" of supernatural love? Or has his ordeal absorbed him in the gravity of the "shut-eyed blank of underearth," so that he has lost all sense of where and who he is—"Is there distance in his head"? Heaney's pointed use of the word "distance" is revealing. In her essay "The Love of God and Affliction," Weil stressed the almost fathomless distance between God and mankind imposed by God's abdication from creation: "the distance between the necessary and the good is the distance between the creature and the creator" (1997, 158). The distance or void, which can only be bridged by the supernatural love manifested in Jesus, is the measure of the value of human suffering:

> As for us men, our misery gives us the infinitely precious privilege of sharing in the distance placed between the Son and the Father. This distance is only separation, however, for those who love. For those who love, separation, although painful, is a good, because it is love. Even the distress of the abandoned Christ is good. There cannot be a greater good for us on earth than to share in it. God can never be perfectly present here below because of our flesh. But he can be almost perfectly absent from us in extreme affliction. This is the only possibility of perfection for us on earth. That is why the Cross is our only hope. (Weil 1951, 127)

If we imagine ourselves in Kevin's place, as the speaker invites us to, and then consider the questions raised in the poem, we might eventually be led to ponder the meaning and value of *any* action in the world, whether it has any absolute value here or beyond the earth—a question we will see Heaney pose elsewhere in "At Banagher" and "Keeping Going." Kevin's posture recalls Weil's emphasis on negating willpower and submitting to the void. In this sense, his stance and actions might suggest that *all* actions, however apparently insignificant, can be sacramental and therefore have absolute eternal value. What is clear, however, is that the questions Heaney poses are meant to lead us to consider the mystery of the self's relation to an invisible God who nevertheless, as Heaney said in his interview with Miller, knows our inmost thoughts.

By raising these questions about the saint's interior state, Heaney undercuts the simple hagiographic legend by focusing on the inner *mystery* of Kevin's action in relation to the metaxu. In one sense, the speaker credits the saint's action as an example of Weilian decreation:

> Alone and mirrored clear in love's deep river,
> "To labour and not to seek reward," he prays,
>
> A prayer his body makes entirely
> For he has forgotten self, forgotten bird
> And on the riverbank forgotten the river's name. (lines 20–24, 1998, 384)

The monk seems to have forgotten his link to the *metaxu* and entered a mystical state, as Daniel Tobin has argued; he seems indeed to occupy Weil's "third dimension" of supernatural love (Tobin 1999, 290–92). Yet Weil herself admitted that such moments of mystical transcendence are very rare: "Man only escapes from the laws of the world in lightning flashes. Instances where everything stands still, instants of contemplation, of pure intuition, of mental void, of acceptance of the moral void. It is through such instances that he is capable of the supernatural" (1997, 56).

In Heaney's poetic version of the legend, St. Kevin *may* enter the mystical state and escape the gravity of the world through decreation, but the self-conscious speaker—and the reader—certainly do not. Rather, Heaney emphasizes the inherent mystery of the situation by balancing the possibility of mystical transcendence against the inquisitive, earthly voice of the speaker and by not attempting to answer the pivotal questions. By rewriting the legend from inside the mind of a modern seeker for meaning, Heaney creates the kind of "double-consciousness" and "inclusive consciousness" he has argued for as defining characteristics of full poetic awareness in our time. Incarnating mystery is the poet's way of redressing the imbalance toward either a rational empiric view at one extreme or a piously romantic view of the saint at the other.[12]

On another level, it seems clear that "St. Kevin and the Blackbird" can also be read as a reflexive poem about the making of poetry itself. As such, it reveals Heaney's attempt to balance the mystery of grace manifested in Kevin's action against the contemporary mind of the speaker viewed as skeptical "historical man," as Milosz called him. More precisely, I believe it reveals Heaney's own complex religiopoetic consciousness as it confronts an age "imbalanced" by those forces of skepticism and positivism that undermine traditional religious beliefs. Apropos this point, it is significant that in his Nobel Prize lecture Heaney described his own early obedience as a poet to the laws of gravity, "the weight of the world," as a time when he wrote poems that dutifully recorded events like a "monk," one "constrained by the rule to repeat the effort and the posture." He confessed that in those years he was "attending insufficiently to the diamond absolutes," until he "straightened up" and began to "make space in [his] reckoning for the marvelous as well as the murderous" (1998, 423) In these comments Heaney identified himself with St. Kevin and saw the saint's care of the fledgling blackbird as a sign of faith, like the poet's writings, manifested "at the intersection of natural process and the glimpsed ideal, at one and the same time a signpost and a reminder." In the Nobel lecture Heaney held up St. Kevin's story as an emblem of poetry itself, because it manifests "that order of poetry which is true to all that is appetitive in the intelligence and prehensile in the affections" (424).

Heaney's linking of St. Kevin's story to the poet's work is particularly revealing. Like the saint, the poet decreates the ego-self humbly before the world and accepts necessity in order, hopefully, to receive the grace of numinous vision, as Heaney said in his interview with Miller. Kevin's love and care for the blackbird becomes an image of the poet's loving regard for the world, the love of the natural world, which is for Weil one of the signs of God's presence. As Robert Frost said of poetry in "The Figure a Poem Makes," "The figure is the same as for love" (1963, 1–4). But unlike Kevin, the poem's speaker is *consciously* examining the meaning of the action through the lens of modern experience with all its implied questions and doubts about its ultimate meaning and the dimensions of love. It is as though, taken as a whole, the poem asks the reader to imagine being a self-aware, questioning Kevin, one committed to the ideal but still bound to gravity—to the pain, suffering, and doubt of our experience in the actual world. For Heaney, hope and the glimpsed ideal are tethered to imagination, to reimaging inherited traditions, as he does in the poem and as the speaker calls the reader to do—imagine being Kevin. Again, to be "of present use," thought and belief must not remain locked in inherited legends, tropes, and actions but must always be revitalized through the transforming power of imagination and language. Heaney's poem enacts such a transformation, and it stands as a model for both poet and reader of a loving posture toward creation that is the antithesis of the acquisitiveness we saw earlier in "Sybil."

Suffering Beauty

As the previous discussion suggests, "St. Kevin and the Blackbird" raises profound questions about the meaning of the saint's suffering, about love, and, by extension, about the mystery of the relation between suffering and the imaginative transformations possible in art. Heaney tackled these knotty issues again, particularly that of suffering, in a tribute to a fellow artist in "To a Dutch Potter in Ireland." In that poem, based on the Dutch poet J. C. Bloem's "After Liberation," Heaney affirms art's redemptive power in the face of the catastrophe of World War II and the Holocaust. Out of the suffering of the war the potter's art has been born. Daniel Tobin sees Heaney's affirmation in the poem as a response to and rejection of Theodor Adorno's famous claim that "there can be no art [*sic*] after Auschwitz" (1999, 278).[13] But Tobin does not address the deeper metaphysical and aesthetic questions raised by the poem; for example, the meaning and "justification" for human suffering in relation to belief in a transcendent order and justice and the relation between such suffering and the beauty of art. Weil's perspective sheds some penetrating light on these questions and on Heaney's poem.

As Katherine T. Brueck has shown, in Weil's view the beauty of art, truth, the good, and transcendent justice are inextricably linked to human suffering. Weil believed that affliction is a manifestation of God's love, the purpose of which is to effect decreation and detachment in the sufferer so that his attention becomes concentrated on the source of truth, goodness, and beauty—the divine being. Affliction calls for a reciprocal response of love from the victim. Rightly understood and accepted, human suffering affirms the cosmic order and divine justice in the universe. In fact, for Weil divine justice is "an attribute that actually requires a world where innocent suffering is a serious and genuine reality" (Dunaway and Springsted 1996, 113). Weil believed that:

> At the origin of the world, God surrenders himself to necessity, a force indifferent to the good and therefore foreign to our nature. By creating the world as a force blind to the good, God, himself all good, enables the human being to return God's perfect act of self giving with a perfect self-emptying act of his own. . . . Only the searing work of affliction, a function of necessity, can call forth a love without flaw. (111)

Characteristically, Weil focuses her metaphysic of suffering on the exemplary model at the center of the universe, the crucified Christ. For her, Jesus's submission to his Father's will and acceptance of gravity to the point of death supremely manifests the inner relation between suffering and supernatural love. Paradoxically, then, for Weil Jesus's cry of abandonment—"My God, my God, why have you forsaken me?" (Matt. 27:46)—is not a cry of despair but of victory, because "the perfect, though hidden love which these only apparently despairing words contain constitutes the secret of both goodness and truth. All forms of authentic beauty, including beautiful art, point in some way to this loving cry" (110–11). Weil believed that the mystery of the relation between divine love, the universal order, and suffering can only be grasped by those who can view affliction from such a transcendent perspective.

For Weil, the artistic genius, especially the tragic poet, is best able to apprehend and express this mystery of transfigured human suffering. Her primary examples are Homer's *The Iliad*; Shakespeare's *King Lear*; Sophocles's *Oedipus Rex* and *Antigone*; and Racine's *Phedre*. Yet closer to home, setting aside Weil's particular focus on the self's relation to God and to Christ's crucifixion, we find a similar general perspective on suffering and the universal cosmic order expressed by W. B. Yeats. Heaney explained and endorsed this perpective in his important essay "Joy or Night: Last Things in the Poetry of W. B. Yeats and Philip Larkin," an essay that is directly relevant to the view of suffering and art Heaney develops in "To a Dutch Potter in Ireland" (1995, 146–63).

In his essay Heaney contrasts the view of "last things" in Yeats's "The Cold Heaven" and "The Man and the Echo" to Larkin's signature poems, "Aubade" and "High Windows." In Larkin's poems Heaney finds a worldview that rejects "any false hope of transcending or outfacing the inevitable"— death. The view is summed up in Larkin's somber lines:

> Courage is no good:
> It means not scaring others. Being brave
> Lets no one off the grave. Death is no different whined at than withstood.
>   (Heaney 1995, 155)

In contrast, Heaney finds that Yeats's "The Cold Heaven" expresses the "metaphysical need" of one who stands nakedly before the frigid expanse of the cosmos and yet summons the courage to face his life-worn imperfect soul and affirm an ultimate meaning for existence. Though Yeats does not affirm a personal God, Heaney argues that in "The Cold Heaven" the speaker's "spirit still suffers from a sense of answerability, of responsibility, to something out there" (148–49). Yeats is concerned with the traditional notions of "the soul's destiny in the afterlife, the consequences in eternity of the individual's actions in time." Those are concerns that Heaney believes indicate "Yeats' embrace of the supernatural" order of reality (150). Gripped by terror and regret, Yeats's speaker is nonetheless "riddled with light" as he asks of his soul:

> . . . when the ghost begins to quicken,
> Confusion of the death-bed over, is it sent
> Out naked on the roads, as the books say, and stricken
> By the injustice of the skies for punishment?

As Heaney points out, Yeats's ending is open-ended, leaving the speaker and the reader faced with metaphysical mystery. Nevertheless, Yeats is resolutely unwilling to "shirk the spiritual intellect's great work" of attempting to comprehend and express the human condition, however tragic, to the fullest measure. Heaney insists that "The Cold Heaven" is a poem "that suggests that there is an overall purpose to life; and it does so by the intrinsically poetic action of its rhymes, its rhythms, and its exultant intonation. These create an energy and an order which promote the idea that there exists a much greater, circumambient energy and order within which we have our being" (149). In defiance of all logic and reason, Yeats embraced supernatural mystery without

any illusions about the gravitational pull toward death, and his unwilling-
ness to foreclose on the mysteries enabled him, as he said, "to hold in a single
thought—reality and justice" (150). His commitment to supernatural purpose expresses a secret suprarational hope in, and implicitly a commitment
to, belief in cosmic order and meaning and the value of suffering for revealing
such larger meaning and for expressing it in art.

In contrast, Heaney argues that Larkin's later poems express a negative
"certainty" about the meaning of existence and therefore refuse any openness
to mystery or hope. The window to the transcendent is blackened. Larkin's
certainty is of a cosmic void, as in,

> the thought of high windows:
> The sun-comprehending glass,
> And beyond it, the deep blue air, that shows
> Nothing, and is nowhere, and is endless. (152)

The only consolation available in the face of the void is to be found in human
kindness. Any attempt to find larger meaning in life is irrational delusion. For
Heaney, Larkin's "Aubade" reneges on the job of doing "the spiritual intellect's
great work," unlike Yeats's speaker, who exhibits a heroic courage and defiance
in the face of suffering and doubt that is the equal of Shakespeare's Lear and
Sophocles' Oedipus or Antigone. It is the courage, defiance, and spiritual victory Yeats's imagined in his magnificent poem "Lapis Lazuli," where Hamlet
and Lear and Ophelia and Cordelia play out their tragic roles without whining, and in the beauty of art reveal "gaiety transfiguring all that dread." Yeats's
poems, for Heaney, manifest a heroic love of a universe ruled by necessity
but informed by a secret meaning beyond human reason, a universe in which
suffering plays a central role in transfiguring gravity into beauty, in life as well
as in art. Furthermore, Heaney connects the aesthetic and ethical imperative
that poetry be "of present use" when he notes that Yeats was determined "to
establish the crystalline standards of poetic imagination as normative for the
level at which people should live" (157). As Heaney said: "he wanted people
in real life to emulate or at least to internalize the fortitude and defiance
thus manifested in tragic art" (157). Such a view of art's power to face up to
human suffering and transfigure it is the shaping vision in "To a Dutch Potter
in Ireland."

Heaney's poem is a parable of hope and recreation, a celebration of the
artist's power to transform necessity and suffering into beauty. The central
image of the potter and pottery making echoes the biblical image of God
the creator as a potter who molds the universe and ultimately shapes human
destiny. Heaney does not make such an analogue explicit, of course, but like

Yeats, his poem affirms a cosmic order and meaning that transcends the tragedies of history. Here, poem making and pottery making are the celebratory
acts, alike in their ability to transform the metaxu of nature and history through
a creative force underwritten by the power of love. Heaney's proem shows the
essential unity of poet and potter as artists. The speaker tells how he

> . . . *entered a strongroom of vocabulary*
> *Where words like urns that had come through the fire*
> *Stood in their bone-dry alcoves next a kiln*
>
> *And came away changed, like the guard who'd seen*
> *The stone move in a diamond-blaze of air*
> *Or the gates of horn behind the gates of clay.* (lines 1–6, 1996, 2)

Poet and language both undergo a purifying trial by fire. Heaney's complex
use of biblical and classical allusions in the proem links the transformative
power of language to the experience of supernatural revelation, to "resurrection," and to artistic self-discovery. "I entered . . . and came away changed."
Self and word are transformed, transmuted through revelation and the fire
of imagination, quickened into the new life of poetic vision and form, like
the transformation of clay into urn. These conjoined images—death and
resurrection, passage through fire, recreation—govern the movement of the
poem as the speaker metaphorically journeys through the inferno of war and
suffering to the "liberation" and renewal signified by the potter's and the
poet's art.

As in many of his poems, Heaney imagines poetic development as a personal journey from the prereflective innocent world of childhood, through
the sufferings of contemporary history, and then beyond to affirm a "glimpsed
ideal" of cosmic order and meaning that is grounded firmly in the actual.
The speaker first recalls his discovery of clean "Bann clay," the "true diato-
mite," which is like "the earth's old ointment box." Like poetry itself, the
clay that becomes the potter's creative medium is associated with healing.
Earth, air, water, and, later, fire are the primordial generative elements, linking the poem's action to cosmogenic myth. Originally, the speaker imagines
the Dutch girl as a "nymph of phosphor" (a source of light) swimming in the
Norder Zee, one he might have known in that "Cold gleam-life under ground
and off the water," and yet an ordinary girl with whom he

> might have done the small forbidden things—
> Worked at mud-pies or gone too high on swings,
> Played "secrets" in the hedge or "touching tongues"—

but did not because of the disastrous war that engulfed Europe. Grim necessity and evil shattered the benign prereflective childhood world he imagines.

Instead, Holland became an infernal cauldron as "night after night" bombers rained down fire and destruction on the land. All Europe became a kiln crematorium, from London to Dresden to Auschwitz. Yet out of this catastrophe both potter and nation

> Came backlit from the fire through war and wartime
> And ever after, every blessed time,
> Through glazes of fired quartz and iron and lime. (lines 31–33, 5)

Despite the catastrophe of war, the speaker's faith and hope remain vested in the human spirit's indestructible capacities for renewal, in life and in art. His faith in the eternal goodness of being is expressed in a brilliant fusion of the primal elements—earth, air, fire, and water:

> And if glazes, as you say, bring down the sun,
> Your potter's wheel is bringing up the earth.
> *Hosannah ex infernis.* Burning wells.
>
> Hosannah in clean sand and kaolin
> And "now that the rye crop waves beside the ruins,"
> In ash-pits, oxides, shards, and chlorophylls. (lines 34–39, 5)

In both idea and form, the movement here imitates the down-up-down rhythm of the movement of gravity and grace that Heaney found so distinctive and salutary in Herbert's poetry. Moreover, viewed from a metaphysical perspective, it imitates the spiritual dynamic of suffering and spiritual victory that Weil saw manifested in the beauty of great art. For her, we recall, beauty in art is "A double movement of descent: to do again, out of love, what gravity does," a movement she called "the mirror of grace" and then asked: "Is not the double movement of descent the key to all art?" (1997, 206).

In the second section of the poem, "After Liberation," the speaker celebrates the freedom and hope imaged forth in "bright-shining spring" when "broad daylight / Swings open" and "the everlasting sky / Is a marvel to survivors." Images of light abound; a "pearly clarity" bathes the fields as "war rumbles away / In the near distance." Survivors like the potter and the poet are now "free to give / Utterance, body and soul"—free to create again. Like Weil and Yeats, the speaker affirms how beauty can spring from suffering and triumph in art. In the image of the potter Heaney sees and presents a universal pattern of the constancy of nature's beneficence and the heart's courage to face up to tragedy and transcend it. His vision echoes Yeats's affirmation of supernatural order, and against necessity, in "A General Introduction to My

Work," "The Cold Heaven," and "The Man and the Echo" (1995, 146–64). In this vision, fear is unwarranted, the speaker says, especially the fear that paralyzes the spirit and destroys hope:

> Turning tides, their regularities!
> What is the heart, that it ever was afraid,
> Knowing as it must know spring's release,
> Shining heart, heart constant as a tide?
>
> Omnipresent, imperturbable
> Is the life that death springs from.
> And complaint is wrong, the slightest complaint at all,
> Now that the rye crop waves beside the ruins. (lines 55–62, 6–7)

What complicates the poem and aligns it with Weil's paradoxical vision is Heaney's suggestion that the catastrophe, the recovery, and the freedom to create may all be part of some transcendent design. The suggestions are carried by his repeated use of religious images: the "diamond-blaze" of air and the guard at Jesus's empty tomb; the "heaven-sent" and "blessed time" after each bombing; the paradoxical biblical phrasing ("*Hosannah ex infernis*" = Praise from / Save us from, the inferno?); the "everlasting sky"; "the life that death springs from"; and "complaint is wrong." Like Weil, and Yeats in "Lapis Lazuli," Heaney's accent is on the spiritual victory and beauty that emerges from tragedy, symbolized by the potter's life and art. In a powerful affirmation of the goodness of *this* life and this world, here and now, he rejects the complaining Larkinesque vision of despair and defeat and presumably any view that would see the war, horrible as it is, as *only* a confirmation of the absurdity of creation. Complaint is "wrong" not simply because, in the cycle of events, peace returns after war, but because Larkinesque whining refuses to embrace the real possibility of the "glimpsed" transcendent order that Yeats and Heaney both affirm and manifest in the action of their poems. Like Weil and Yeats, Heaney looks to a larger universal pattern in which suffering is ultimately transfigured by knowledge and hope, by the unafraid heart "knowing as it must know spring's release," and by recognizing and affirming "the life that death springs from." In the universal order of things, life undergirds death. Heaney exhibits what the poet Edwin Muir called "the feeling for a permanence above the permanence of our human existence" (1977, xxi). That such a vision comes through suffering and loss is the fundamental mystery the poem presents, without evasion or rationalization. Heaney's affirmation of a universal order and meaning *despite* catastrophe and suffering is a testament to his metaphysical and poetic faith. The potter herself—and her work—testifies to such faith, especially since so many of her contemporaries were, if not physically destroyed, spiritually crushed by the war. She exhibits that "courage" of the heart and mind that Weil found in King Lear and Oedipus when they rose from the ashes of their degradation to finally comprehend and accept the underlying truth of human frailty and the need for love that comes through suffering.

We can see Heaney's focus clearly in the way he "revisions" Bloem's poem to emphasize the larger pattern of the relation between suffering, vision, and art. Bloem wrote:

AFTER LIBERATION

I
Beautiful and radiant, just like then, is the spring
Cold of morning, but as the days open up
Further, the eternal light is a miracle
For those who have been saved.
In the transparent haze upon the fallow
Land plow once again the slow workhorses.
As always, even as the nearby distances
Rumble with war.
To have experienced this, to say this
with body still whole, every time awakening again
To know it: it is over, and now forever, the almost
Unbearable servitude—
Worth it it was, to have languished for years,
Now rising up, then giving in again, and not
One of the unborn shall ever grasp
Freedom in this way.

II
Regular measure of the returning seasons!
What is the heart that has ever feared,
Knowing spring would come to liberate it,
Radiant as it has ever been.
Even in the present, indestructible
Life that flowers out above death,
And the smallest of complaints seems barely audible
Where the rye above the ruins grows.[14]

In contrast to Bloem, Heaney first situates the poem's subject within his personal myth of creative development and then emphasizes the triumph of art over gravity's inexorable power—here, the force of war. He shifts the focus of the poem to the creative power of the artist, both potter and poet, to move through tragedy and create anew. In addition, he develops the immediate subject—reprieve from the suffering of war—within a larger natural and metaphysical pattern of order, a pattern in which the artist's power of imagining and reimagining experience affirms the fundamental goodness and beauty of the world. Thus Heaney's vision is more emphatically optimistic and hopeful, making it one of his strongest affirmations of the indestructible power of art and a testament to "the spiritual intellect's great work."

Heaney's emphasis in "To a Dutch Potter in Ireland" on the power of the artist—poet, potter, craftsman—to transform the forces of gravity through love, work, and imagination obviously contravenes Weil's general proscriptions against imagination. While she acknowledged the importance of the metaxu, of work, of earthly beauty and tragic art as a mirror of the invisible God, her ideal spiritual modus vivendi demanded a stripping away of the egoistic self and a detachment from the world. As we saw, for her the true counterbalance to necessity is an *imitatio Christi*, a self-effacement and obedience to the law of gravity that opens one, potentially, to the gift of grace. Yet as Thomas R. Nevin and others have suggested, Weil's paradigmatic Christ is in some measure a self-reflecting image of her own sacrificial life. As we saw, in her emphasis on Jesus as solitary victim, she truncated the historical person of Jesus, ignored his bodily resurrection, and consequently deemphasized the glorified Christ. Because of this, Weil tended to undercut the theological basis for notions of hope and transformation that might be possible *within*, not beyond, a world seen as dynamic process. In short, as Thibon and Panichas have argued, Weil undercut the full meaning of the Christian redemptive vision and thereby diminished the possibilities of grace through human action within the metaxu of the ordinary world (Weil 1997, 32–34).

Furthermore, the ethic of decreation and purification of the self Weil demanded, with its admonitions against concern with either past or future, its stricturess against imagination, and its austere view of human friendship, demands a *kenosis* that runs counter to the actual experience of complex consciousness in the experience of the modern world. (We saw such a state of kenosis in the ending of "St. Kevin and the Blackbird": "For he has forgotten self, forgotten bird / And on the riverbank forgotten the river's name.") This reality of complex, conflicted mind is the condition of gravity and deformation that I described earlier. Because of it the mind is often turned away from the transcendent good and left to struggle constantly in the field of gravity. Heaney's spiritual allegiance is with those engaged in that struggle. Still, the development of what he calls "inclusive consciousness" and of poetic imagination can be transforming forces within that struggle. For him, poetry has ethical consequences when it truthfully shows that complex consciousness fully engaged in life's struggle and at the same time suggests openings to the transcendent. As he said in his essay "Joy or Night," when "a poem rhymes, when a form generates itself, when a meter provokes consciousness into new postures, it is already on the side of life. When language does more than enough, as it does in all achieved poetry, it opts for the condition of overlife and rebels at limit" (1995, 158). In contrast to Weil's emphasis on decreation, Heaney argues that "the truly creative writer, by interposing his or her perception and expression, will transfigure the conditions and effect thereby what I have been calling 'the redress of poetry'" (2002, 356).

For Heaney, then, pushing against and redressing the gravity of what has happened (the past) and what is actually happening (the present) demands an imaginative transformation of those conditions so as to produce a new awareness and way of seeing events recorded in the poem. The artist is the quintessential transformer; yet paradoxically, as we have argued, his power of vision depends upon a "displacement" from actual and remembered events to command the kind of detached pure attention and comprehensiveness of vision that Weil would certainly endorse. Again and again in his poems Heaney dramatizes the struggle of a consciousness striving to be inclusive and to transform the forces of gravity. This struggle is at the heart of his richly dense lyric, "Damson."

Building Memory

The speaker in "Damson" initially recalls a specific memory from childhood, which then serves as a focal point for his struggle over the repercussive associations—personal, historical, and mythical—which the memory stirs up. For Weil, as we saw, memory (the past) is paradoxical. On the one hand, it is part of each individual's metaxu; therefore, it serves as an analogue of the pure supernatural. But on the other hand, as an active force in consciousness, it exercises a gravitational pull that can distract the mind from focusing on the ascent to purity and goodness in the present. For Heaney, memory also possesses an ambivalent power; it is both defining and restricting, as illustrated in his poem "The Settle Bed." Recalling his inheritance of a childhood bed, an emblem of Northern Ireland's constrained past, the speaker says:

> Then learn from that harmless barrage that whatever is given
> Can always be reimagined, however four-square,

Plank-thick, hull-stupid and out of its time
It happens to be. (1998, 321)

Moreover, in commenting on the speaker in Derek Mahon's poetry, Heaney argued that the poet must create a space "not just by moving out of Ireland but by evolving out of solidarity into irony and compassion. And, needless to say, into solitude" (2002, 131). His remark is applicable to much of his own work, certainly to "Damson." Here, the speaker first recalls how as a child he saw a bricklayer/housebuilder with his right-hand knuckles bleeding from a scrape. He associates the dark blood of the wound with the stain of damson plum seeping through the bricklayer's packed lunch, and these memories of wound and stain and damson trigger other memories both salutary and grim. He remembers taking pleasure in the sheer craft of the bricklayer as he sets down mortar and brick with meticulous precision. But the blood and plum stain also awaken the imagined ghosts of assailants and house stormers and victims in Ireland's sanguinary history, who reappear now to claim a hold on the speaker's consciousness, threatening to undermine the salutary power of his recollection.

These antipodal memories of building and destroying can be read, of course, as images of universal historical conditions, past and present. In one sense, the house is the house of Ireland or even of civilization itself, still under construction by wounded laborers and still open to assault by shadowy figures hell-bent on absorbing the present and future into the past. But more importantly, these opposing recollections focus the struggle in the speaker's mind, so that the struggle is over how to sustain a constructive view of reality that can be both true to history's brutalities and yet open to the hopeful ideal of trustworthy human community. In short, it represents the mind of the poet engaged in his struggle. Stated differently, "Damson" raises the particularly Irish but nonetheless universal question of whether it is possible to shape human consciousness toward a more enlightened and humane future, given the wounds of history and the so-often mortifying power of memory. The question is at the heart of the speaker's struggle, and by being true to itself as a poem—in form, image and dramatic movement—"Damson" is true to Heaney's hopeful sense of the possibilities of enlarged vision and a better future.

On another level "Damson" is also concerned reflexively with the craft of poetry itself, as is so often the case in Heaney's poems. House building and house mending—the house of art, as it were—are figuratively associated with poetry and the development of poetic consciousness, as in his earlier poems "Thatcher" and "Alphabets." Here, the bricklayer's craft can be seen as an emblem of the writer's craft in its linearity, its order, its precision in making "lines," and the risks or "wounds" attendant upon such activity. Later in the poem Heaney amplifies the metaphor by envisioning the bricklayer as a king or builder called upon to drive back the "bloody" ghosts of the past that threaten the house, not with weapons of violence—sword or spear—but with the builder's instruments—trowel (line maker) and "mortar board" (shield, knowledge, craft). The poem interweaves acts of making in complex ways—making walls and houses, making war, making sacrificial rites (Odysseus), making plum jam, and reflexively, making the poem itself. (One etymology of the poem's first word, "gules," traces it to the word for throat.)

The poem opens with the blunt, cryptic phrase—"Gules and cement dust"—that sets the terms for the speaker's struggle over vision. Heaney's use of the term "gules," with its heraldic, armorial associations, situates the speaker's memory of the bricklayer within a context that opens into the past—his childhood memory of seeing the wounded bricklayer and, by extension, his imagining of the bricklayer now as some wounded warrior or lord defending his castle walls. The heraldic "gules" suggests a past tradition defined by noblesse and class distinction, by a code of honor based on heredity, fealty, and tribal justice; by allegiance and revenge; and by vicious tribal warfare as the preeminent means of establishing and maintaining identity and solidarity within the system. The poem's first word, then, establishes the past as a gravitational force within the speaker's mind, pulling him, as it were, to see the bricklayer and his bleeding hand within an imagined context shaped *entirely* by historical and mythological precedents. (Weil would likely have regarded this as precisely the danger of imagination—a distraction from the spiritual "present" of the bricklayer.)

But the second half of the opening phrase—"and cement dust"—counterbalances the memorializing weight of the word "gules." Cement dust has all the grit of the ordinary, of metaxu, of the quotidian present rather than the heroic past, and of common labor rather than lordly battles. As he so frequently does, Heaney here shifts the context of words and meaning by a process of defamiliarization that opens the way to new meanings, a strategy that undergirds the mystery and movement of the poem. Taken together, the two halves of the opening line create the force field that the speaker must traverse as he imagines and reimagines the poem's title word: "damson." Several questions are implicated by the opening line. How will the speaker see the meaning of the bricklayer's injury and the plum stain in light of the contradictory associations it provokes? More importantly, what meaning will he fathom from his memory of the bricklayer as an instance of how to define and imagine the present? How will he balance the conflicting elements in consciousness and still be open to the undefined future? Indeed, to see the memory *only* in terms of a heraldic tradition would be a stoic acceptance that would close consciousness to new awareness and fresh associations.

After setting the contending polarities in the opening line, the speaker recalls the sight of the bricklayer at the time of his injury:

> A full hod stood
> Against the mortared wall, his big bright trowel
> In his left hand (for once) was pointing down
> As he marvelled at his right, held high and raw:
> King of the castle, scaffold-stepper, shown
> Bleeding to the world. (lines 4–9, 1998, 380)

He imagines the bricklayer as like a wounded, vulnerable king, with the instrument of his craft held useless in his left hand, not the hand a king would use to wield a sword. In his mental equation of king and bricklayer, of lord and laborer, of past and present, the speaker sees the bleeding bricklayer against the backdrop of the unfinished wall as if the whole scene were a heraldic tableau that might be represented on a crest or shield. But the vision is threatening. This memory from childhood has stirred up a deeper and more ominous awareness of a heroic, brutal age of power and violence that could, if allowed, be predictive and determinative of the future. So Heaney ends the first section of the poem with the speaker contemplating how the force of memory lives and shapes the present:

> Wound that I saw
> In glutinous color fifty years ago—
> Damson as omen, weird, a dream to read—
> Is weeping with the held-at-arm's-length dead
> From everywhere and nowhere, here and now. (lines 10–14)

Yet while the past threatens to constrain the present, it must nonetheless be recognized and interpreted—"a dream to read"—and then reenvisioned. Apropos this need, the speaker assumes the role of interlocutor, as Odysseus did when he held the dead at arm's length in the underworld in order to gain foreknowledge of his future.

Section 2 of the poem counterbalances the first section as the speaker recalls a more benign memory of the bricklayer at work and his own joy in observing the bricklayer's craftsmanship:

> Over and over, the slur, the scrape and mix
> As he trowelled and retrowelled and laid down

Courses of glum mortar. Then the bricks
Jiggled and settled, tocked and tapped in line.
I loved especially the trowel's shine,
Its edge and apex always coming clean
And brightening itself by mucking in. (lines 15–21)

Although the trowel is "heavy as a weapon" and "like a cult blade," there is "no strain" when the bricklayer uses it; "it was all point and skim and float and glisten." The trowel is a tool for building and joining, not for conquest and division. But allusions to weapons and cult blades suggest that the sanguinary past and its hold on memory are not so easily overcome. The dead are ever-present in memory and ready to assert their power over the present. The speaker must confront and transform the "wounded" past. Only in this process can his recollections of bricklayer and damson—these mental metaxu—finally become the instruments of transforming vision.

Section 3 opens with the threat of the all-consuming past, the history of violent conquest, asserting its force:

Ghosts with their tongues out for a lick of blood
Are crowding up the ladder, all unhealed,
And some of them still rigged in bloody gear. (lines 22–24)

The fusion of images here, as in the speaker's mind the ladder becomes the instrument for bloody "ghosts" to storm a castle, suggests conflicting possibilities of vision. Confronted by this grim vision, the speaker calls upon the bricklayer to rout the ghosts back into the past:

Drive them back to the doorstep or the road
Where they lay in their own blood once, in the hot
Nausea and last gasp of dear life. (lines 25–27)

Initially, the speaker associates the bricklayer's commanded action with that of Odysseus in Hades:

Trowel-wielder, woundie, drive them off
Like Odysseus in Hades lashing out
With his sword that dug the trench and cut the throat
Of the sacrificial lamb. (lines 29–31)

The reference here is to book 11 of *The Odyssey*, when Odysseus visits Hades to gain knowledge of his future from Tieresius. He is forced to confront the ghosts of the past: dead warriors like Achilles; women, lovers of gods and humans; and the mothers of warriors, including his own. Heaney's specific allusion is to the sacrificial rite Odysseus must perform in order to "assuage

the nations of the dead." Odysseus digs a votive pit with his sword and sacri-
fices a lamb and ewe, filling the pit with their blood. Immediately the souls
of the dead rush forward,

> brides and young men, and men grown old in pain,
> and tender girls whose hearts were new to grief,
> many were there, too, torn by brazen lance heads,
> battle stain, bearing still their bloody gear. (Fitzgerald 1998, 186)

Odysseus grows "sick with fear" and draws his sword "to keep the surging
phantoms from the pit" until he can be sure Tieresius is present. As the
speaker commanded earlier in the poem, Odysseus holds the encroaching
dead "at arm's length," even the shade of his mother Antikleia. He grieves at
the sight of her and his dead fellow warrior Elpenor, killed when he missed a
ladder and fell from Kirke's roof. Odysseus keeps them at bay until Tieresius
arrives, tastes the blood and then begins to "speak true" about Odysseus's
future. Tieresius prophesizes the hero's eventual return home to Ithaca but
only after many trials and the loss of his ship and crew. And even when he
reaches home, Odysseus must face the suitors and slaughter them to "make
those men atone in blood" (Fitzgerald 1998, 188). Finally, after the ghost of
Tieresius fades, many other souls come to enlighten and advise Odysseus—
including his mother Antikkleia, plus Antiope, Jocasta, Leda, Agamemnon,
Achilles, and others. Odysseus's journey to Hades brings him an enlargement
of vision and foresight, a glimpse of the spirit world beyond the earth, and a
dramatic representation of his past, present, and future.

   But the speaker's brief, momentary association of the ordinary bricklayer
with the heroic raider of cities, of damson stain with the blood of ritual sacrifice, is finally not honorific. The Odyssean model, while it credits the mythic
truth of the past and must be attended to, is finally not adequate to the vision
Heaney wishes to affirm in "Damson." It is not adequate, he suggests, to
our present or future reality, and so not of present use. To be sure, Odysseus
returns home to the loving arms of Penelope, but his slaughter of the suitors
only perpetuates the cycle of violence and revenge, the cycle of history when
it merely recapitulates the past, from which there is no escape in Homer's
epic, where culture is define by tribal solidarity, honor, and revenge.

   Therefore, the speaker in "Damson," surrogate voice of the poet, retracts
his initial association of the bricklayer with Odysseus. Heaney redirects the
poem's focus toward a more enabling vision, as in the ending of "Mycenae
Lookout." After having recalled Odysseus's sacrificial act, the speaker sharply
differentiates bricklayer from warrior:

But not like him—
Builder, not sacker, your shield the mortar board—
Drive them back to the wine-dark taste of home,
The smell of damsons simmering in a pot,
Jam ladled thick and steaming down the sunlight. (lines 32–36)

The speaker calls upon the builder to drive the ghosts back to the originating source of human community—the "home" where the deepest human capacities for love and trust can fructify. Just as the damson plums are transformed into jam, the speaker/poet transfigures the experience from an ominous recollection of violence, the wounds of memory, into a more nourishing vision to carry into the future. The nourishing image of home used here suggests how a memory can further consciousness and the future. It is an example of what J. M. Baker Jr. demonstrated to be a Weilian "moment of nostalgia"—the soul's longing for the ideal embodied in the actual object in the metaxu, in the metaphysical unity of subject (seer) and object (thing).

As "Damson" reveals, for Heaney imaginative consciousness can serve as the instrument for redressing the imbalance caused by the gravity of events, past and present. He does not share the real fear of imagination and memory that Weil so often expressed, despite her metaphysic of "nostalgia" regarding the past. More characteristic is her austere outlook, as when she said: "The imagination is continually at work filling up all the fissures through which grace might pass . . . the imagination, filler up of the void, is essentially a liar," and that we "must continually suspend the work of the imagination filling the void within ourselves" (1997, 62–64, passim). Although several of Heaney's poems, such as "Clearances VIII" and to some degree "St. Kevin and the Blackbird," focus on the experience of the void, as a poet, he obviously rejects Weil's rather cramped view of imagination. Her way of renunciation, while essential for mystical ascent to God, diminishes the actual experience of ordinary, complex human consciousness in the present; that is, the way in which the mind's fluid activity is shaped by the many-layered, asynchronic flow of impressions, memories, thoughts, and imaginings. Past, present, and imagined future coalesce with near simultaneity both within the mind and in the mind's relation to the flow of external events. Moreover, as we saw, Heaney insists on the "double consciousness" of the poet in the act of creating, the play of mind engaged simultaneously in presenting the subject of the poem and in the self-conscious act of poeticizing itself. Heaney's poetic use of time, memory, and imagination is far more organic and earthbound, more directly engaged in the metaxu than Weil's penchant for abstraction, her asceticism, and her striving for mystic transcendence normally allow.

"Two Lorries," for example, reveals such a complex consciousness as a force field of memory, imaginings, nostalgic longing, and dread. In this beautiful sestina, the speaker initially recalls a childhood scene in which a coalman named Agnew, while making a delivery, is "sweet-talking" his "nineteen-forties mother" about going to "a film in Magherafelt." The scene is redolent of flirtation and, for a country wife, the romance of going to town to see a movie, the "dream of red plush and a city coalman" as the mother thinks: "And films no less! The conceit of a coalman." As the speaker recalls the event from his childhood, the scene may also be somewhat disconcerting, to see a city coalman "sweet-talking" his mother about going to the movies. The dusty coalman, with his banter evoking the "dream of plush seats," may hint at a symbolic lover-death figure, a role Agnew assumes in the speaker's vision at the end of the poem.

After recalling the childhood scene between his mother and Agnew, the speaker's memory quickly melds into a horrifying recollection of a later time when the town's bus station is blown to bits by sectarian bombers:

> Oh, Magherafelt!
> Oh, dream of red plush and a city coalman
> As time fastforwards and a different lorry
> Groans into shot, up Broad Street, with a payload
> That will blow the bus station to dust and ashes. (lines 19–23, 1998, 378)

This grim memory provokes a vision of his now-dead mother as a revenant sitting in the waiting room with her "shopping bags full up with shovelled ashes." The flirtatious coalman Agnew suddenly metamorphoses into the figure of Death,

> Refolding body-bags, plying his load
> Empty upon empty, in a flurry
> Of motes and engine-revs.

The imagined vision of his dead mother shatters the earlier memory of flirtation, forcing the speaker to question which is real—farmyard flirtation, reprisal bombing, or mother as revenant. Heaney's transformation of key motifs, of actuality and "dream," blurs the distinction between actual events and the illusory, as indeed consciousness does. Moreover, his use of cinematic images—"film," "fastforward," "groans into shot"—underscore the melding of dream and actuality in the speaker's mind. Like the querulous speaker in "St. Kevin and the Blackbird" when he questioned the saint's inner self, this speaker asks:

> which lorry
> Was it now? Young Agnew's or that other
> Heavier, deadlier one, set to explode
> In a time beyond her time in Magherafelt. (lines 25–28)

The question is the pivotal point in the poem. It is a question any self-conscious person faces in trying to negotiate between memory, dream, and actuality in the process of self-definition. But more broadly, it is a question to be faced by modern society, especially in Northern Ireland: Is it to be the ordinary life with dreams of romance and love, perhaps illusory? Or is it to be violence and fratricidal killing? Or more broadly, what is the relationship between fate and freedom? Heaney's focusing of the speaker's consciousness on the present—"which lorry / Was it *now*?" (emphasis added)—creates that "riff" in time between "what is going to happen and what we would wish to happen" that Heaney earlier ascribed to the action of poetry itself. "Two Lorries" counterbalances the weight of actual events—Agnew's flirting, the bombing of the station, and the dream-vision of his mother as ghost—against the speaker's supple transformation of Agnew from actual coalman into the figure of Death, a dreamboat Charon, and then back again into an imagined lover:

> So tally bags and sweet-talk darkness, coalman.
> Listen to the rain spit in new ashes
>
> As you heft a load of dust that was Magherafelt,
> Then reappear from your lorry as my mother's
> Dreamboat coalman filmed in silk-white ashes. (lines 35–39)

The movement of the sestina is circular, as actual and imagined events are circumscribed within the speaker's mind. In the ending, the coalman "filmed in silk-white ashes" is imaginatively revivified as "dreamboat" lover, recalling the actual Agnew and his "tasty" talk of films in the opening stanza. Finally, the speaker reimagines both memories—coal delivery and bombing—and turns them into an expressed hope, a glimpsed ideal that may be illusory, for the triumph of love over death. However, the speaker's Weilian "moment of nostalgia" is counterbalanced by the tough ethical choice for the future stated in the pivotal question the speaker asks:

> Which lorry
> Was it now? Young Agnew's or that other
> Heavier, deadlier one, set to explode.

Rephrased, the question becomes: which way of life is it to be in the future?

Walk on Air

Despite her generally negative view of imagination, Weil did believe that works of creative genius can provide inspiration that "tends—as Plato said— to make us grow wings to overcome gravity" (Panichas 1977, 295). At the same time that she insisted on the importance of the metaxu and on the need to submit to gravity, Weil believed that works of genius can point the way to transcendence, as Kathleen Brueck has shown. Heaney's "The Gravel Walks" develops this theme of "transcending" gravity in paradoxical fashion by celebrating the interpenetration of spirit and matter within the metaxu. Viewed from a philosophical perspective, the poem is a metaphysical exegesis on how the spiritual dimension of reality or glimpsed ideal is firmly embedded within actual realities. This interpenetration is manifested in the mysterious "in-between" quality of the poem. Near the end of the poem the speaker echoes Weil and Plato by exhorting the reader to "walk on air against your better judgement." But the title of the poem, and the scene depicted, counterbalance such a gravity-defying, suprarational act; rather, they suggest an earthbound passage of transcendence *through* the metaxu. Thus the journey to be taken, in consciousness as well as in fact, incorporates all the major dichotomies of life in the metaxu: actual/imagined; spirit/body; past/present; and temporal/eternal.

River gravel is the lodestone image that focuses all these dichotomies. It was present, the speaker states, "in the beginning," at the original source of life. Heaney's use of the Johannine biblical phrasing suggests that the substance is primordial, an element in the creation at the beginning of time and history. The spirit world is also evoked at the outset when the speaker recalls questioning the "ghost" of an angler recently encountered on the walk. River gravel partakes of both "worlds," physical and spiritual. It is a solid, earthly substance but, symbolically, a principle of higher truth whose "plain, champing song against the shovel / Soundtests and sandblasts words like 'honest worth'" (line 20, 1998, 395). Its "champing song," like that of poetry itself, measures realities ranging from prehistoric and mythical times down through history to the present. It perdures from the time when "the engines of the world" began, down through the Tantalus-like world when "green nuts / Dangled and clustered closer to the whirlpool," and through the preconscious innocent and timeless world of children playing in water,

> an eternity that ended once a tractor
> Dropped its link-box in the gravel bed
>
> And cement mixers began to come to life. (lines 4–5, 11–13)

Heaney's speaker suggests that obedience to the law of gravity, the world of brute fact, without the counterforce of spirit and imagination, is a form of captivity and slavery. Tantalus is trapped in Hades, forever unsatisfied, and punished by the gods for his murderous impiety. The cement makers work "like captive shades . . . as if / The Pharoah's brickyards burned inside their heads," their minds locked into monotonous routine. But for those with imaginative double vision, like the speaker, bits of gravel are "Gems for the undeluded. Milt of earth" and a "verity" to "Hoard and praise" (lines 16–18). Heaney invokes a vision of spiritual freedom from earthly enslavement, a vision proclaimed by Jesus and St. Paul, when the speaker says:

> The kingdom of gravel was inside you too—
> Deep down, far back, clear water running over
> Pebbles of caramel, hailstone, mackerel-blue. (lines 22–24)

Heaney's affirmation of the "kingdom within," the kingdom of light, echoes philosopher Owen Barfield's insight about Jesus's claim that the "kingdom of heaven" is within. Barfield says that the phrase refers to the revolutionary transformation by which the Logos—the divine spirit of truth—comes to reside, not in external law, but within human consciousness and imagination. Commenting on the parable of the sower and the seed, Barfield says:

> The parable . . . was about the sowing of the word, the Logos, in earthly soil. It was an attempt to awaken his hearers to the realization that this seed was within their own hearts and minds, and no longer in nature or anywhere without. . . . Henceforth the life of the image was to be drawn from within. The life of the image was to be none other than the life of imagination. And it is of the nature of imagination that it cannot be *inculcated*. There must be first of all the voluntary stirring from within. (1965, 178–79)

The kingdom of gravel, then, stands as a vital symbol of the metaxu, a sign of the transcendent principle of spirit lodged in the actual world where "salvation" in the sense of the full realization of human nature must be worked out. Escape into false transcendence, without pain, is foreclosed, as

> the actual washed stuff kept you slow and steady
> As you went stooping with your barrow full
> Into an absolution of the body,
> The shriven life tired bones and marrow feel. (26–28)

Here, Heaney rejects the idealism and dualism of Plato, instead affirming an incarnational vision that is both Christian and, insofar as she affirms spirit in the metaxu, Weilian. Body, instead of soul, is absolved and shriven. In the end the speaker urges the reader to, like the visionary poet, "walk on air against your better judgement," i.e., follow the law of the spirit of transcendence while living within the mystery of the metaxu, just as poetry itself "stops" time and lives within the "riff" between ideality and actuality:

> Establishing yourself somewhere in between
> Those solid batches mixed with grey cement
> And a tune called "The Gravel Walks" that conjures green. (lines 30–32)

Heaney's statement about poetry as a "riff" in time reveals that, for him, the goal is to help redress the age's imbalance by creating a "space" of suspension, attention, and waiting, as a way to recall us to an awareness of our true place in the order of being, our true relation to the transcendent. For Heaney and for Weil, the creative genius—philosopher, poet, sculptor, potter, musician—is best able to express this vision of reality. And as both Yeats and Wallace Stevens affirmed, poetry can indeed show us how to live.

Weil condemned modern society's failure to nourish such attention to our true spiritual being, i.e., to a belief in the metaphysical unity of spirit and matter that enables us to transform gravity. She saw most of her fellow citizens as trapped in a condition of slavery, benumbed by the distractions of materialism and soul-destroying work in a collectivized economic order:

> To make an inventory of our civilization—what does that mean? To try to expose in precise terms the trap which has made man the slave of his own inventions. How has unconsciousness infiltrated itself into methodical thought and action? To escape by return to a primitive state is a lazy solution. We have to discover the original pact between the spirit and the world in the very civilization of which we form a part. But it is a task which is beyond our power on account of the shortness of life and the impossibility of collaboration and succession. *That is no reason for not undertaking it.* The situation of all of us is comparable to that of Socrates when he was awaiting death in his prison and began to learn to play the lyre. . . . At any rate we shall have lived. (1997, 210; emphasis added)

Seeing Chair

Weil's reference to the condemned Socrates as an emblem of "the situation of all of us," i.e., faced with the gravity of mortality yet attracted to the glimpsed ideal represented in art, points to the "riff" in time Heaney creates and celebrates in his delightful lyric "Poet's Chair." The poem, dedicated to the chair's maker, sculptor Carolyn Mulholland, honors the artist's commitment to the ideal represented in sculpture and poetry, an ideal often manifested in varied and often whimsical emanations. In the proem, the speaker records Leonardo's observation that the sun, symbol of divine being, *"has never / Seen a shadow,"* and then notes how the sculptor analogously represents that divine power within the metaxu.

> *Now watch the sculptor move*
> *Full circle round her next work, like a lover*
> *In the sphere of shifting angles and fixed love.* (lines 1–3, 1998, 398)

Observing the chair and its "angling shadows" in a "sun-stalked inner-city courtyard," the speaker celebrates its quirky uniqueness:

> On the *qui vive* all the time, its four legs land
> On their feet—cat's-foot, goat-foot, big soft splay-foot too;
> Its straight back sprouts two bronze and leafy saplings. (lines 4–6)

The chair is available for all to use,

> Every flibbertigibbet in the town,
> Old birds and boozers, late-night pissers, kissers,
> All have a go at sitting on it some time. (lines 11–13)

Then, in an amusing thrust at Yeats's ideal of metamorphosis and artifice in "Sailing to Byzantium," the speaker adds:

> Once out of nature,
> They're going to come back in leaf and bloom
> And angel step. Or something like that. *Leaves*
> *On a bloody chair! Would you believe it?* (lines 16–19)

Section 2 of the poem shifts to a new angle of vision as the speaker sees

> the chair in a white prison
> With Socrates sitting on it, bald as a coot,
> Discoursing in bright sunlight with his friends. (lines 20–22)

Facing immanent death, he nonetheless proclaims a vision of the transcendent.

> Socrates
> At the center of the city and the day
> Has proved the soul immortal. (lines 32–34)

But the speaker focuses on the immediate temporal-spatial metaxu, rather than on philosophical discourse. His attention to the details of Socrates' final minutes creates a poetic riff, one of those "moments of nostalgia" that links present (sculpted chair in Dublin) and past (Socrates' death), and then concentrates into a revelation of being:

> The bronze leaves
> Cannot believe their ears, it is so silent.
> Soon Crito will have to close his eyes and mouth,
> But for the moment everything's an ache
> Deferred, foreknown, imagined and most real. (lines 30–34)

In the final stanza, the angle of vision becomes personal as the speaker-poet recalls himself sitting, like Socrates, "all-seeing / At centre field, my back to the thorn tree," watching his father plow a field (lines 36–37). The focus here is on celebrating the "all-seeing," foreknowing vision of the artist-to-be, the kind of near-omniscient vision that embraces the present moment, the actual and ideal, and the power to transform them into poetry, a power whose source, Heaney suggests, is love of the transcendent divine reality:

> I am all foreknowledge.
> Of the poem as a ploughshare that turns time
> Up and over. Of the chair in leaf
> The fairy thorn is entering for the future.
> Of being here for good in every sense. (lines 39–43)

Earlier I cited Weil's argument that the conditions of modern life have made man "the slave of his own inventions," the result of which is that "unconsciousness [has] infiltrated itself into methodical thought and action" (1997, 210). Unconsciousness is the opposite of "attention," the latter which Weil equated with prayer, as we saw (1951, 105–16). Slavery and unconsciousness mean a subservience of *mind* to the force of gravity, a thwarting of the need to attend to the transcendent ideal. What is needed, as Weil said, is a way "to discover the original pact between the spirit and the world in the very civilization of which we form a part." Weil and Heaney both suggest that Socrates' learning to play the lyre on his deathbed shows a mind ever attentive to the original pact between spirit and the world. But how to recover this capacity? Heaney, as we saw, argues that consciousness can be reshaped by imagination, that is, by the free exercise of a mind that resists the "slavery" of conformity to inherited views and narrowly mundane circumstances. The mind saturated with mundane concerns to the exclusion of all else cannot achieve the needed detachment to imaginatively rethink actualities and counterbalance them with a vision of the possible ideal. But the actual process of realizing this liberation of mind is a difficult one, as many poems in *The Spirit Level* reveal. As for poetry-making itself, for Heaney it always involves a difficult passage through the metaxu, physical and mental, the complex and fluid states of mind shaped by memories, dreams, fears, hopes, and the consciousness of personal responsibilities. Compounding the difficulty is the poet's sense of, as Heaney called it, his "double-consciousness of his role as both citizen and artist," of his obligation to verify what happens ("how it was") and to express what Weil called "the original pact between the spirit and the world," without in any way slighting the autonomy and freedom of the poem as a work of art. We can see the difficulty of this struggle in consciousness and Heaney's attempt to circumscribe it poetically in one of his most complex renderings of that struggle, "Keeping Going."

Double Vision

Early in his career Heaney sounded a major chord in his oeuvre when he said, quoting Yeats: "poetry is out of the quarrel with ourselves and the quarrel with others is rhetoric" (1980, 34). Heaney's persistent quarrel with himself is an energizing frisson in his poems, as "Keeping Going" clearly reveals. Many critics, notably Helen Vendler and Daniel Tobin, have pointed to the biographical and historical dimensions of the poem, which is a tribute to Heaney's brother Hugh, who, unlike the poet, stayed to live and work as a farmer in Northern Ireland (Vendler 1998, 156, 164, 175; Tobin 1999, 280–81). Heaney honors his brother's quotidian life of perseverant work and good will. Hugh is a benevolent presence amidst the brutalities and murders that are indelible bloodstains in the history of the Derry community. In honoring his brother as a figure of enduring and generous humanity, Heaney balances the horror of a part-time reservist's assassination against the recollected pleasures of childhood as he remembers Hugh's imitation of a bagpiper marching his happy siblings through the family home. In this sense, the poem can be seen as a down-to-earth Yeatsian dialogue between "gaiety" and "dread."

Without denying the obvious biographical dimensions of the poem, I believe that on another important level it dramatizes the poet-speaker's own self-scrutiny as he attempts to weigh, balance out, and poeticize contradictory pulls within his own mind and heart. On this level the poem depicts what Heaney has spoken of as "the way consciousness can be alive to the contradictory dimensions of reality and still find a way of negotiating between them," a way of "furthering" consciousness (to use Heaney's term), or what I would call a way of poetic "keeping going." The "contradictory dimensions" in the poem are the speaker's recollected and imagined worlds, on the one hand, and the present actual world, on the other, both of which interpenetrate and clash in his mind as he struggles to negotiate between them. In this respect, the figure of "Hugh" in the poem can be seen as a double or alter ego of the speaker, that is, an aspect of the speaker's own potential being, personified as a force in the unfolding drama of poetic self-realization. Heaney's deliberate blurring of clear distinctions between the imagined and actual worlds, his metamorphic transformation of key images and tropes, and his use of time shifts as the poem registers its complex movement between memory and external action all justify such a reading. As much as being a literal tribute to his brother, "Keeping Going" is a poem that "takes place," as it were, within conscious-ness, a dialogue between self and soul about those matters of poesis and poetic responsibility that have preoccupied Heaney throughout his career.

The opening section of the poem (lines 1–8) pictures Hugh, the speaker's alter ego, at childhood play, imitating a piper with a "whitewash brush for a sporran" and "a kitchen chair / Upside down on your shoulder," marching brothers and sisters through the house. As Daniel Tobin has pointed out, in Heaney's poems play is a form of "imaginative self-extension," one which can "offer an ethical alternative to violence in the civilizing nature of its play" (1999, 281–82). Play for Heaney becomes a metaphor for imaginative cre-ation. Commenting on the ending of Frost's "Directive," where Frost con-trasts an imagined children's playhouse with the actual "house in earnest," Heaney says "that the games of make-believe which the children played in the playhouse were a kind of freely invented answer to everything in the 'house in earnest' where . . . life was lived in sorrow and anger." Heaney sees that Frost's metaphors create a parable about poetry itself, so that the entire poem becomes a parable of the journey to poetic self-realization:

> Frost suggests that the imaginative transformation of human life is the means by which we can most truly grasp and comprehend it. What Virgil called the *lacrimae rerum*, the tears of things, can be absorbed and re-experienced in the playthings of the playhouse—or in the words of the poem. . . . The poem reveals "a fleeting glimpse of a potential order of things, 'beyond con-fusion,' that has to be its own reward." (1995, xv)

For Heaney, the poet's self-discovery is bound up with negotiating the two dimensions of reality, for "it is in the space between the farmhouse and the playhouse that one discovers what I've called 'the frontier of writing,' the line that divides the actual conditions of our daily lives from the imaginative rep-resentation of these conditions in literature" (xvi). Such is also the case with the speaker's imaginative recreation of "Hugh" as a music-maker, marching his siblings around in a play that is a mocking counter step to the destructive sectarian "marches" in the actual world of the Derry culture.

Negotiating the space between "contradictory dimensions of reality," between imagined and actual, is achieved through poetic transformation. Consequently, the real mystery of "Keeping Going," I believe, lies in the way Heaney interweaves, fuses, and transfigures the two planes of consciousness as the speaker moves through the experience of his own mind engaging, shaping, and reshaping those realities as part of a process of self-understanding. So the second section of the poem (lines 9–23) opens with the actual whitewash brush, the ordinary object no longer used as a "sporran," as it was in section 1. It is just an "old, blanched skirted thing / On the back of the byre door," yet a tool with strangely premonitory powers associated with the world of magic, evil, and dread. The brush was

> biding its time
> Until spring airs spelled lime in a work-bucket
> And a potstick to mix it in with water.

Heaney suggests a kind of double time whereby the brush exists in two realms, since the "spelled" lime and potstick anticipate the witches of *Macbeth* who appear in section 4 of the poem to cast their own spell upon the fated hero. But here, the "actual job" of mixing the lime "brought tears to the eyes" as "we inhaled / A kind of greeny burning and thought of brimstone."

Heaney's evocation of the other world of magic and mystery in the impressionable mind of his youth as they prepared the lime foreshadows the deeper questions about "the meaning of it all" that the speaker will ask at the end of the poem, the great cosmic mystery of existence. Yet even the actual work of brushing walls with fresh lime possesses its own transforming power. As they watch the walls "drying out / Whiter and whiter, all that worked liked magic." Whether such whitewashing will have the power to efface or transfigure the bloodstains of murder, whether the "world-renewing potential of the imagined response" will be adequate to redress "the social one," is a question Heaney implicitly raises in the opening double action of play and work in the poem. And for the speaker and his alter ego "brother," the double action opens a deeper epistemological question about the very dimensions of reality, of origins and meanings. The speaker asks: "Where had we come from, what was this kingdom / We knew we'd been restored to?"

The question suggests the possible restoration of a lost kingdom, perhaps like Frost's recovery of the source of imaginative life in "Directive" or the primordial "kingdom within" referred to in "The Gravel Walks." It also suggests an intuitive knowledge of origins in another "world" or plane of reality, a true "place" or frontier of being from which to know and measure the actual world. The notion is reinforced when the speaker says,

> Our shadows
> Moved on the wall and a tar border glittered
> The full length of the house

—as if they now inhabit an in-between, metaxu world marked by "a black divide / Like a freshly opened, pungent, reeking trench." The trench antici-pates the gutter and the reservist's brutal murder in section 5. But as in "Dam-son," it also suggests, in the poet-speaker's mind, his imagined "descent" into the underworld of classical literature, the blood-filled trench of sacrifice where the shades of the dead congregated before Odysseus.

That underworld fuses with the actual world in the opening of section 3, when the speaker recalls how "the dead will congregate" at night at the gable of the house. As Helen Vendler has noted, Heaney evokes here the pre-Christian Irish world of superstition (1998, 165). Yet in the context of the poem, this evocation of pagan Ireland is set within the larger question of the relationship between actual and imagined realms and of the possibility of an ideal order that is "beyond confusion." Though the allusion to pagan ritual may suggest the tribal killings committed in fact and memorialized in myth in Northern Ireland, and thus foreshadow the murder of the reservist, the night world here is eerily peaceful:

The only time the soul was let alone,
The only time that face and body calmed
In the eye of heaven.

Ordinary, actual time is framed against the backdrop of eternal peace—"the eye of heaven." So the scene looks backward to the timeless "kingdom" evoked in section 2 and forward to the question posed at the end of the poem: "Is this all? As it was in the beginning, is now and shall be?"

The speaker must negotiate the two realms. While he recalls the out-of-time world of childhood when we "were all together in a foretime," he fears that such a world

might not translate beyond
Those wind-heaved midnights we still cannot be sure
Happened or not.

He questions what is real, what extends beyond the actual. Which is the true kingdom: the actual childhood world? the world of adult responsibility? the imagined world? the kingdom to come? The different worlds meld and inter-twine in the speaker's consciousness. But his premonitions of a world of pain and suffering are realized when his brother breaks his arm and he shares "the dread," marked by an ominous "strange bird" perched on the byre roof.

That "dread" of evil becomes palpable in section 4, when the speaker identifies with "Macbeth helpless and desperate / In his nightmare." What was once the imagined play of his brother's piping in section 1 now becomes a nightmare vision of the dread-filled play in Shakespeare's tragedy. Transformations of earlier motifs abound. The bucket for mixing lime to whitewash the house now becomes the "hags'" pot where "apparitions" are conjured to foretell the disaster and retribution Macbeth cannot escape. Recognizing the play of evil in "that scene," the speaker says that he "felt at home with that one all right." Home is no longer a joyful haven, as his memory of the hags' warning to Macbeth recalls his mother's warning to avoid "bad boys / In that college that you're bound for." But her warning is powerless to save him from an intimate knowledge of evil. His own nightmare vision is identified with that of Macbeth. The gruel which was a nourishing pap in childhood becomes the poisonous gruel stirred by the hags with a potstick. And now the adult speaker tastes the bitter gruel of memory. The killings and revenge forecast for Macbeth by the witches become the speaker's own dread-filled vision of future disaster with

> everything intimate
> And fear-swathed brightening for a moment,
> Then going dull and fatal and away.

The "nightmare" vision of section 4 suggests how the imagined world of play dissolved from joyous childhood music-making into the imagination of disaster in the speaker's memory of Shakespeare's tragedy. The killing and revenge in *Macbeth*, given order and significance through the language and art of Shakespeare's play, are countered by the grim and "senseless" actuality of the reservist's assassination in section 5. Just as helpless to change "what happens" as Macbeth was in his nightmare, the speaker imagines the fatal event. The gruel of childhood pap and the witches' brew become the "grey matter" of exploded flesh "flecked with blood / In spatters on the whitewash." The wall, refreshed and renewed in the annual ritual of whitewashing, "subsumed" the bloodstains over time. But the stains of violence and sectarian reprisal cannot easily be subsumed or whitewashed from his memory. As he identified with Macbeth in the dread of his nightmare, the speaker now identifies with the casual unnamed victim. "And then he saw an ordinary face / For what it was and a gun in his own face." The tarred border that "glittered / The full length of the house" in section 2 becomes the "tarred strip" where the murder victim falls, "Feeding the gutter with his copious blood." Images of nourishment ("feeding") and sacrifice crystallize in the cruel ritual of revenge that mocks the "magic" kingdom of childhood, where a whitewash brush could be transformed imaginatively into a sporran to create the "music" of joyful play.

"Keeping Going," then, can be read as a poem about self-scrutiny and the process of self-actualizing through imagination and language. Viewed in this way, the figure of "Hugh" can be understood, as I have said, as an alter ego of the poet-speaker as he negotiates between the imaginative and actual realms of reality. One piece of evidence for this, it seems to me, is the fact that as a literal figure, "Hugh" largely disappears from the poem in sections 2–5. In those sections, the speaker explores what Heaney has referred to as "the country of the mind," the complex, dynamic world of memory, language, and imagination out of which the poem came to be fashioned. Viewed from this perspective, the figure of "Hugh" is present throughout the entire poem as a representative of the ordinary, quotidian world, like the ordinary unnamed reservist and his killer. As an alter ego, he challenges the poet-speaker to "make sense" of such a world and to measure the meaning of such a life in terms of ultimate realities. In short, the brother-self confronts the speaker with fundamental questions about *his* life and chosen vocation, and about his obligation to the quotidian world vis-à-vis his art. Again, the poet must negotiate the true "space" between the fateful actualities of history and the transforming power of art.

In the last section of the poem the actual "Hugh" appears again as an image of endurance and steadfastness in the face of history's brutal realities. As such, he represents the poet-speaker's own fidelity to the gravity of the actual world, the ordinary quotidian experience. Hugh is a benevolent communal spirit who pulls his tractor into the Diamond—the site of the reservist's assassination—waves at people, and shouts and laughs above the sound of the engine. In these actions he serves as an emblem and reminder of the bonds that unite, rather than divide, the community. As the speaker says, "you keep / Old roads open by driving on the new ones"—as indeed the poet's art also does. But there is another reality beyond the quotidian, seen when the speaker again recalls the childhood world of imagined play: "You called the piper's sporran whitewash brushes / And then dressed up and marched us through the kitchen." Heaney's syntactical reversal—Hugh's calling the piper's sporrans whitewash brushes instead of the opposite—suggests the fusion of the two realms, actual and imaginary. Nevertheless, the poet must acknowledge the limits of imaginative power to change the brutal facts of experience by some definitive transformation. Hugh as "musician" can vivify their humanity and create joyful play, "but [he] cannot make the dead walk or right wrong." He is neither God nor Christ; injustice and murder persist. As Heaney has remarked, no lyric poem ever stopped a tank.

Nevertheless, the poet has the power to imagine another order of reality in his work, an ideal point of light and reference for judging "what happens." In a statement quoted earlier, Heaney pointed to the "unlimited" power of the poet's words to "verify our singularity." As we recall, he compared the poem to Jesus's writing in the sand and then said, "in the rift between what is going to happen and whatever we would wish to happen, poetry holds attention for a space, functions not as distraction but as pure concentration, a focus where our power to concentrate is concentrated back on ourselves."

In the end of the poem Heaney turns to confront both the limits and possibilities of art. In this self-questioning, he again balances the contrary pulls of actuality and imagined alternative, in particular by posing the whole matter as an impenetrable mystery. The speaker sees his brother Hugh "at the end of your tether sometimes . . . holding yourself up . . . until your turn goes past." Hugh has suffered a spell, an ironic echo of the "spell" he cast over the children with his imitation of a piper in childhood, as well as the spells cast by the hags in *Macbeth*, or indeed the spell cast by the poem itself. When he comes to himself again "in the smell of dung" he wonders: "is this all? As it was / In the beginning, is now and shall be?" The question circumscribes all time and is, of course, Heaney's abridged version of the Christian prayer that affirms eternal glory: "As it was in the beginning, is now, and *ever* shall be, world without end, Amen" (emphasis added). But the speaker poses it as a question, not as a fact, and significantly, he omits the word "ever" from the original phrase, leaving the mystery of "is this all?"—the mystery of whether there is any possible order beyond the actual world—unresolved. And though cast in the brother's mind, the question is clearly that of the poet-speaker himself, since it is the question about the limits and boundaries of reality and art that he must face again and again in the self-scrutinizing process of writing, as Heaney noted in his essay "Frontiers of Writing" (2002, 186–203).

In the last view we see of Hugh in the poem, he stands as a figure of endurance, a faithful attendant to the ordinary matters of the everyday world, doing "the decent thing": "Then rubbing your eyes and seeing our old brush / Up on the byre door, and keeping going." But the "rubbing your eyes" again suggest the poet's sense of double vision, harkening back to the lime mixing that brought "tears to the eyes" in section 2 and to the spell of vision cast by the witches in *Macbeth*. The poet *knows* that the world of seeing and being are mysteriously intertwined, and that what "might be" imagined is both real and a cause for wonder. It is this special power of double vision that enables the "keeping going" of art in the face of things. Heaney's speaker and alter ego brother are both aspects of the poet's self and of poetic imagination's response to experiences that begin with an ordinary lime brush and then are transfigured through art into an inclusive vision of our truest state of mind, and thus our most humane selves.

In paying tribute to his brother Hugh's durable and enduring life in "Keeping Going," Heaney tips the balance between gravity and grace toward honoring those forces of necessity—"the decent thing" of personal and communal obligation—that both define and constrict his brother's life. While intimations of transcendence are present in the speaker's reflective consciousness and in his own growth into the different life of a poet, the poem ends by posing a question about the absolute value of the quotidian life: "And wondering, is this all? As it was / In the beginning, is now and shall be?" The ultimate answer to the mystery still remains beyond the reach of mind or art.

Outward Bound

While "Keeping Going" may tip the balance between the actual world and the imagined ideal in favor of gravity, still, "grace" is manifested in the art of the poem—the brilliant transformation of images and the dynamic rhythm of lines that carry the reader into the flow of consciousness and action as the poem unfolds. These elements counterbalance the somber subject and tone of the poem. In "The Swing," in contrast, the balance is more even-keeled. The poem is another of Heaney's parables of growth, of weighing the balance between gravity and grace, between down-to-earth necessity and the aspiration to transcend. The thematic rhythm of the poem hinges on the action signified by the poem's central metaphor, the swing itself. The swing operates in the metaxu, moving between earth and sky, actual and ideal. As an ordinary plaything, the swing both bears weight and, with effort, defies gravity as the rider pumps arms and legs to rise above the ground. So also does the speaker's imagination work through a complex of symbolic associations—personal, historical, mythical, and religious—to create a dynamic rhythm between the ideal and the actual. In a poem that echoes Robert Frost's "Birches" and "After Apple-Picking," as well as Herbert's "The Pulley," Heaney, like them, strives to incarnate the glimpsed ideal within the down-to-earth ordinary world.

As the speaker understands its symbolic significance, the swing was their instrument of growth, whereon "Sooner or later, / We all learned one by one to go sky high." Like a pendulum, it marks the time of development, the rite of passage from childhood to maturity. In the speaker's mind it is partly associated with the transcendent ideal. But unlike the pastoralized ideal in Fragonard's frothy painting *The Swing*, it is

> more
> Hans Memling's light of heaven off green grass,
> Light over fields and hedges. (lines 8–10, 1998, 400)

Light suggests grace, and so the barn where the swing hangs is a scene reminiscent of "a Nativity / Foreground and background waiting for the figures." Yet the swing is ordinary and unidealized, "the swing itself / With an old lopsided sack in the loop of it," but also (an echo of Herbert's "The Pulley") a possible bridge to the transcendent, "hanging like pulley-slack, / A lure let down to tempt the soul to rise" (lines 15–17).

Nevertheless, the youthful soul's aspiration to go "sky high" is countered by the gravitational pull of earth, specifically the tie to the earth-mother figure in the poem, who sits like an "empress," bathing her swollen feet. While the speaker recalls how they all "favoured the earthbound," he also recognizes how constrained and constraining the earth-mother's life has been by her faithful submission to the duties and cares of the actual world. The "light of heaven" associated earlier with the swing is now absent from her very ordinary experience:

> Whatever light the goddess had once shone
> Around her favourite coming from the bath
> Was what was needed then: there should have been
> Fresh linen, ministrations by attendants,
> Procession and amazement. Instead, she took
> Each rolled elastic stocking and drew it on
> Like the life she would not fail and was not
> Meant for. (lines 26–33)

Tempted once to sit in the swing, she agrees, but she sits motionless and alone, thinking perhaps of another life once aspired to or dreamed of, but never realized, "half-retrieving something half-confounded." Like the brother Hugh in "Keeping Going," she has faithfully done "the decent thing."

The quest to transcend limits, to leave the earth-mother and go "sky high," evokes the mythic pattern of growth from childhood to maturity, but such a quest inevitably entails a plunge into history and down-to-earth hard realities. (Heaney's comparison of the scene to a Brueghel painting in line 8 may suggest the latter's famous painting *The Fall of Icarus*.) As imagination and the light of grace inspire thoughts of flight, gravity restrains and qualifies aspiration. Retrospectively, the speaker acknowledges this necessity. In the final stanza, Heaney balances the two possible dimensions of reality, yet still affirms the aspiration. The gain in knowledge is offset by the cost in pain and partial disillusionment. The child world of play once graced with the "light of heaven" is now gone. The "townlands vanished into aerodromes" (for war), and the heavenly light is turned ironically into an image of brutal slaughter—"Hiroshima made light of human bones." The swing is replaced by mechanical flight, "Concorde's neb migrated toward the future." Yet despite such recognition of world-pain, loss, and disillusionment, the passage to maturity brought with it a self-transcendence that fortifies the soul as it faces the world and faces the future:

> In spite of all, we sailed
> Beyond ourselves and over and above
> The rafters aching in our shoulder-blades
> The give and take of branches in our arms. (lines 50–53)

Significantly, in this passage Heaney replaces the earlier image of Jesus's nativity, the divine child about to enter the world, with an image that suggests both entanglement with the world and a kind of symbolic crucifixion, the "rafters aching *in* our shoulder-blades" and "the give and take of branches *in* our arms" (emphasis added). The speaker accepts the world burden and the cost it exacts for maturity. The final vision of transcendence, of moving "beyond ourselves," situates the swing within the down-up-down metaphysical dynamic that Heaney saw at the center of Herbert's religiopoetic dynamic and that Weil saw confirmed in the crucifixion. "The cross as a balance, as a lever. A going down, the condition of rising up. Heaven coming down to earth raises earth to heaven" (1997, 145).

Just as an ordinary plaything in "The Swing" serves as a metaphor for balancing the imagined ideal and the actual, for negotiating the metaxu in a process of growth, so also does an ordinary sofa serve in "A Sofa in the Forties." It recalls Heaney's comment on Frost's "Directive" when he said "that the games of make-believe which the children played in the playhouse were a kind of freely invented answer to everything experienced in the 'house in earnest.'" Heaney compared this dual activity to the making of poetry, we recall, and affirmed that "the playhouse has the measure of the other house, that the entranced focus of the activity that took place as make-believe on one side of the yard was fit to match the meaning of what happened in earnest on the other side, and in doing so Frost further suggests that the imaginative transformation of human life is the means by which we can most truly grasp and comprehend it." Heaney goes on to say that the poem is like the broken drinking goblet dipped in a stream in Frost's poem, a draught that offers "a fleeting glimpse of a potential order of things 'beyond confusion'" because it contains "the clear water of transformed understanding and fills the reader with a momentary sense of freedom and wholeness" (1995, xv).

In Heaney's poem, the sofa imagined as a train, with "the invisible / For tickets," becomes a vehicle for a journey of imagination through the metaxu. A solid, ordinary sofa of black leatherette, it nevertheless possesses an "ornate gauntness" and "airs / Of superannuated pageantry" (1998, 373). To the imagining mind it suggests otherworldly mystery and possibility: "Ghost-train? Death-gondola?" On Christmas morning it is an altar of hope and disappointment, bearing the "insufficient toys." As a symbol, it stands as a metaphysical focal point, a metaxu, at the beginning of life's journey—"Potentially heavenbound, earthbound for sure, / Among things that might add up or let you down" (lines 23–24).

In the third section of the poem Heaney imagines that life journey as a descent into the quotidian world. The speaker says, "we entered history and ignorance." History, the gravity of actual events, is "ignorant" in its blunt resistance to imaginative transformation. Embarked on the imaginary life journey, the passengers are subjected to the mundane, the "news" spoken by an "absolute speaker" using an alien voice in which "pronunciation / Reigned tyrannically." Yet entering "history and ignorance," the metaxu, is a necessary rite of passage. One must experience "the sway of language and its furtherings" and "the abstract, lonely curve of distant trains," real trains that bring with them separation from home and the community: "as we entered history and ignorance."

But in the last stanza of the poem Heaney recalls and recovers the child world of play and the sofa as imagined train. The values affirmed here are fidelity to the imagination and to the tenacious belief in the worth of such imaginings for their own sake, just what poetry itself manifests. Such imaginings, the speaker suggests, are an adequate response to the gravities of pain, separation, and death encountered in the actual world. For the imaginative mind, "constancy was its own reward already." Though the journey may be fraught with difficulties, the riders task is to remain true to the imagined reality: "Our only job to sit, eyes straight ahead, / And be transported and make engine noise."

Implicit in Heaney's claim for imagination's power to counterbalance the gravitational pull of "history and ignorance" in "A Sofa in the Forties" is the intimately mysterious connection he suggests between imagination and grace. The imagination's power to transform the actual is, as we have seen, a sign of the workings of grace in the natural order. If obedience to the law of gravity is "the greatest sin," as Weil said, then resistance to gravity through the grace of imaginative transformation indicates a movement toward liberation of the spirit. Such a movement, however, includes recognizing one's human failings and the need for forgiveness, a recognition often triggered by some seemingly insignificant object or event as the instrument of recognition and grace. Weil insisted upon attention to such apparently small matters, since

she understood attention to be a form of prayer that could help the soul rise
toward the good in life and the ultimate good—supernatural love.

Heaney's beautiful short lyric "Mint" synthesizes all of these interwoven themes into a concise parable of moral reckoning, one that brings the
speaker to a liberated vision by his attention to the disregarded and by his
implicit admission of moral failure. This recognition springs from a humble
attentiveness to the grace of small things. The clump of mint growing wild
behind the house is generally disregarded, "almost beneath notice." Yet in its
wild, free growth the tenacious mint also spells "promise," "newness," and
abundance (1998, 372). In the "light of Sunday / Mornings" when the usually ignored mint is "cut and loved," it triggers a revelation in the speaker's
mind that spans life from beginning to end: "my last things will be first things
slipping from me." In Heaney's revision of the opening line of T. S. Eliot's
"East Coker" ("In my beginning is my end."), personal memory opens into
a *memento mori* and recognition of our failures of attention, which are really
failures to love. As Weil said, the beauty of nature is a manifestation of God's
presence (i.e., his love) in the world. In his recognition the speaker now credits the values of tenacious endurance and hoped-for freedom that are signified
by the wild-growing mint. This revelation inspires a lofty vision of liberation,
triggered by the bracing smell of clipped mint:

> Yet let all things go free that have survived.
>
> Let the smells of mint go heady and defenceless
> Like inmates liberated in that yard.
> Like the disregarded ones we turned against
> Because we'd failed them by our disregard. (lines, 12–16)

The smell of mint evokes this call for absolution and liberation, particularly
for those whom we have twice failed, first in our disregard and then in our
rejection of them, because they remind us of our having failed them. The
speaker's pain of conscience recalls a similar failure recorded in "Weighing
In," but in "Mint" the personal failing is overcome by a humble acknowledgement of guilt and by the imaginative thrust toward freedom of mind and
heart. This uplifting vision comes through the speaker's seeing himself and the
disregarded ones, like the mint, within the eschatological context of first and
last things. Recollection of the mint inspires a metanoia based on recognizing
the need for attention to the "least" things, like the saint and the fledgling
blackbird in "St. Kevin and the Blackbird," and to their redeeming power.
Heaney suggests that when well regarded, the least things can be the vehicle
of grace, of moral accounting, and a liberating renewal of the spirit. Weil's
entire ethic of spiritual transcendence through humble attention is portrayed

in "Mint." In the poem's elusive and paradoxical final lines, Heaney inscribes the real possibility of liberation. Liberation comes by recognition of moral failure, of the gravity of egotism, and of that disregard of others that is a failure of love and a "sin" against the spirit. Hope comes in the recognition of such failure, and for Heaney, it is frequently linked to the notion of freedom. And in "Tollund," this hope for a new spirit of freedom is projected onto a broader and more complex landscape than in "Mint."

Freeing Death

As commentators as well as Heaney himself have pointed out, "Tollund" was inspired by the hope for a better future in Northern Ireland raised by negotiations for a peaceful settlement after the decades of murderous strife. Heaney regards the many years of sectarian bloodshed in the North as a tragic "waste of spirit," a monotonous round of hatred and revenge killings that ground down the entire community. The gravity and somber mood of that situation was captured microcosmically in the brutal sacrificial rites enacted in the bog poems in his earlier volume *North* (1973) and in "The Tollund Man." In that poem, the poet-speaker is astray in an imagined primitivistic Jutland, one of "the old man-killing parishes" not unlike the Northern Ireland of the 1960s and 1970s. He feels "lost / Unhappy and at home," his own dolorous spirit a reflection of the culture's spiritual morass. In contrast, "Tollund" is set within the contemporary Jutland of the modish 1990s, a mixture of the ancient and modern with its "bog-fir grags," tourist signs "in *futhark* runic script," satellite dishes, and traffic sounds (1998, 472). No longer seen as one of the man-killing parishes, it is a "user-friendly outback" that reminds the speaker of John Hewitt's "Townland of Peace," a poem of "dream farms / Outside all contention." Now "things had moved on," so that the speaker and his companion stand "footloose, at home beyond the tribe." No longer constrained by the nightmare memory of killings, he stands ready to move into the future with hope and new spirit.

What also distinguishes "Tollund" from "The Tollund Man" is that the speaker imagines himself and his companion as spirits returning from the ethereal to the terrestrial world. They return to Jutland like "ghosts who'd walked abroad / Unfazed by light." The image recalls Heaney's claim for Northern Irish poets as "the voice from beyond," as imagined visitors or ghosts from some mythical or supernatural realm. Likewise, it recalls Thomas Hardy's imagined voice from beyond his own death in "Afterward," as well as Yeats's Byzantium poems, but with wry and crucial differences. Unlike the purged spirits destined to return to the world in Yeats's myth of reincarnation, Heaney's ghosts return

> to make a new beginning
> And make a go of it, alive and sinning
> Ourselves again, free-willed again, not bad.

They are returning, not as purified souls but as fully human and flawed creatures. Yet they are free to try out the tentative reality of peace with renewed spirit and hope. Transcendence is rejected in favor of the metaxu and the down-to-earth work of making "a new beginning." Paradoxically, here Heaney revises the traditional Pauline notion of sin as slavery and death by granting his revivified returnees the spiritual freedom to choose a better future in this world, not in some afterlife. This new consciousness of being "alive and sinning," which is the most distinctive quality of human freedom, is no guarantee of success. But it does signify a consciousness liberated from the atavisms and gravities that have trapped the culture in the past, that brutal time when the speaker identified closely with the sacrificial victim in "The Tollund Man," riding with his "sad freedom" to his death in the bog.

If Northern Ireland was trapped in the gravity of cyclical, atavistic sectarian violence in the 1960s and 1970s (we recall Weil's observation that evil is repetitiously "monotonous"—1997, 119), then the new reality projected in "Tollund" implies a hope grounded in freely imagining a better future, a liberation of the spirit that might produce a greater realization of our human potential. Thus Heaney suggests a potential evolution of consciousness toward the glimpsed ideal of a "townland of peace," one that is the earthly analogue of the transcendent order. In this suggestion, "Tollund" fulfill his assertion that the fully achieved poem can be "of present use" insofar as it acknowledges both present realities and future possibilities.

The appearance of the speaker and his companion in "Tollund" as "ghosts" returned to life also points to the larger questions of death and immortality and the relationship between them. But beyond imagining this reincarnated state as a trope, Heaney does not explore its implications in "Tollund." As is generally the case in his poems, he situates the poem on the border between death and the unknown and so preserves the impenetrable mystery their "ghostly" status entails. However, this is not the case in "A Dog Was Crying Tonight in Wicklow Also," where the origin of death is presented through the lens of mythic fable.

In writing the poem, Heaney revised an African legend about the origin of death. In the legend, Chukwu, supreme deity of the Ibu people (his symbol is the sun), sends a dog messenger to his people to tell them how to overcome death. When anyone dies, he says, they must place the corpse on the ground and cover it with ashes, and the person will then return to life. But the dog is delayed on his journey; then Chukwu sends a sheep to deliver the message. The sheep is also delayed, stopping to eat; he forgets the message, then guesses at it, telling the people, wrongly, that they should bury the corpse. When the dog arrives later with the original true message, he is not believed, and so death is established on earth.[15]

In his poem, Heaney shifts the point of view from Chukwu the deity to humans; it is they who send a dog to Chukwu to find out how to overcome death and return to the "house of life," like birds returning to "the same old roosts" after a night spent in the woods. But the dog is distracted by another dog barking, and when a toad reaches Chukwu first, he delivers a quite different message: "human beings want death to last forever." Chukwu's mind "reddened and darkened" into a somber vision of death, with people's souls returning in birds to a void—"To a place where there would be neither roosts nor trees / Nor any way back to the house of life" (1998, 405). The dog finally arrives with the correct request, but nothing can change the god's vision. Light is "obliterated," and the shadow of death covers all—"great chiefs and great loves," the toad in mud, and the dog crying "all night behind the corpse house."

Heaney's undercutting of the quest for immortality and his focus on death as the ultimate gravitational force or law of necessity recalls Weil's view of such matters. She said: "Belief in immortality is harmful because it is not in our power to conceive of the soul as merely incorporeal. So this belief is in fact a belief in the prolongation of life, and it robs death of its purpose"(1997, 84). Weil does not say here what the "purpose" of death is, but elsewhere in *Gravity and Grace* she associates it with the need to face the void as a precondition for grace. The void or "dark night" must be established in the self through decreation. "Grace fills empty spaces but it can only enter where there is a void to receive it, and it is grace itself which makes this void." For her, "To love truth means to endure the void and, as a result, to accept death. Truth is on the side of death" (55–56).

Heaney's revision of the Ibu myth affirms that stark reality, and perhaps it can be said that his frequent willingness to face that "void" and write about it truthfully is the graced vision created in his many elegiac poems, all imaginatively written within the perspective of human consciousness, its limited knowledge, and its apprehension of mystery. For example, in "Lightenings I" he imagined the particular judgment as a beggar shivering in a doorway in winter light. The speaker proclaims: "there is no next time round" but only "Unroofed scope. Knowledge-freshening wind" (1998, 322). In "Squarings xliv," he questions the platitudinous phrase *"All gone into the world of light?"* and says:

> Perhaps
> As we read the line sheer forms do crowd
> The starry vestibule. Otherwise
>
> They do not.

And in "Bodies and Souls I," ("In the Afterlife"), he wryly imagines the afterlife as

> like following Jim Logue, the caretaker,
> As he goes to sweep our hair off that classroom floor
> Where the school barber set up once a fortnight. (2001, 88)

Sewing and Herding

Heaney's focus remains steadily on the metaxu, the intermediary reality that fixes our attention on the threshold between earthly things and the transcendent. He finds a special kinship with those figures, often artists and craftsmen, who symbolically represent the "in between," borderline life. In "At Banagher," such a figure is "the journeyman tailor who was my antecedent." This ordinary "self-absenting" tailor is fully absorbed in his mundane task of mending, yet to the poet-speaker he is a figure of mystery, "unopen, unmendacious, unillumined" (1998, 409). Like the speaker in "St. Kevin and the Blackbird," this speaker tries to fathom the tailor's inner mystery yet recognizes that he cannot.

> So more power to him on the job there, ill at ease
> Under my scrutiny in spite of years
> Of being inscrutable as he threaded needles.

Watching the tailor at work, the speaker wonders about the larger mystery of the relationship between the tailor's mundane life of work and its transcendent significance. "Does he ever question what it all amounts to, / Or ever will? Or care where he lays his head?" (lines 21–23). No answer is forthcoming from the unself-conscious "Buddha"-like tailor. Yet paradoxically, he serves both as a sign of the human limits of knowledge and as an intermediary who inspires further explorations into the mystery of the transcendent. So the speaker pays tribute to him as a hieratic figure: "the way / Is opener for your being in it." As Weil said: "All created things refuse to be for me as ends. The world is the closed door. And at the same time it is the way through" (1997, 200).

Heaney's Banagher tailor embodies a central Weilian principle. He represents for the speaker a "contradiction" that is for Weil always the criterion of
the real; yet he is also, symbolically, a "lever of transcendence." Paradoxically, in
his "unillumined" and "self-absenting" meticulous absorption in his trade, he is
an inspiration and an instrument for "furthering" vision. So also is the down-
to-earth figure of Caedmon that Heaney imagines in "Whitby-sur-Moyola,"
where the poet ironically transfigures the divinely inspired poet of legend
into an ordinary Derry farmer. For the speaker, Caedmon as muse is not the
lofty singer whose whole being is concentrated on ethereal heavenly matters.
Instead, he is the "perfect yardman," practicing his "real gift" of feeding
animals and

>   just bogging in,
> As if the sacred subjects were a herd
> That had broken out and needed rounding up. (1998, 397)

He has left his "angel stint" of "poeting with the harp"; his hands join and his
eyes turn heavenward only when he sniffs "a sick beast's water." Caedmon is
"the real thing all right." He is "real" because he inspires the poet to ground
his vision in the actual and again enact Weil's principle that "earthly things are
the criterion of spiritual things" (1970, 147). In his tribute to Caedmon as a
down-to-earth muse he "was lucky to have known," the speaker also "herds
in" the spirit of the legendary divinely inspired singer by imagining him
at the boggy labors of a common farmer. In the speaker's mind, Caedmon
stands "watching you"; he is a criterion to test and verify the poet's commitment to earthly things that are "the real thing," i.e., the criterion of the
transcendent real.

Like Weil, Heaney understands that fidelity to the metaxu, the in-between
world that is both barrier and doorway is also a way of healing the deformed
spirit. In this sense art can be redemptive, offering a way to transcend, albeit
temporarily, the forces of gravity and a way to show us how to live. But this
requires a special kind of interior vision, a power of imagination to accept contradiction and see through the actual to the true source of vision in the transcendent world. For Heaney, the artist best manifests this curative power.

Healing Sight

In "At the Wellhead," another poem that strongly echoes Frost's "Directive,"
Heaney embodies this curative vision in two solitary singers, an unnamed
singer (his wife) and a blind neighbor pianist, Rosie Keenan. Like Frost's signature poem, the double sonnet "At the Wellhead" is a reflexive meditation on

art itself, especially as it relates to the inevitable "gravity" of human solitariness. In the first sonnet the "shut-eyed" singer's song evokes in the speaker the image of her as a lonely figure standing on a country side road where few cars come and go. But the image of journeying then becomes a metaphor for both the artist's and the reader's journey toward healing and wholeness, as in "Directive." The speaker urges his "Dear, shut-eyed one" to "Sing yourself to where the singing comes from," the spiritual source beyond the actual. In her self-imposed "blindness," her attunement to the source, the singer resembles the second "shut-eyed" singer, "our blind neighbour, / Who played the piano all day in her bedroom" (1998, 408). The spiritual source of inspiration, healing, and wholeness is again signified by water, as her music sounds "like hoisted water, / Ravelling off a bucket at the wellhead."

The second sonnet focuses on the blind Rosie Keenan, a figure who embodies all the paradoxical contradictions that the artist must confront and transfigure. She evokes the ordinary and the marvelous, suggested by Heaney's conjoining of opposite images. To the speaker she is

> like a silver vein in heavy clay
> Night water glittering in the light of day.
> But also just our neighbour, Rosie Keenan.

Mysteriously, "her eyes were full / Of open darkness and a watery shine." Limited by her blindness, she nonetheless seems to possess an inner vision of wholeness and the good that is transmitted to others, perhaps like Heaney's "glimpsed ideal" of what art can achieve. Thus the speaker affirms her redemptive power:

> Being with her
> Was intimate and helpful, like a cure
> You didn't notice happening.

What gives this blind musician her curative power? It is the power she possesses, despite physical blindness, to evoke the spirit within material things by her music and to imagine a reality beyond her physical limits. Again, the way through the metaxu to the spiritual source is by imagination. Heaney captures her visionary power in the paradoxical final lines of the poem:

> When I read
> A poem with Keenan's well in it, she said,
> "I can see the sky at the bottom of it now." (lines 26–28)

The movement recapitulates the rhythmic movement of grace. Listening to a poem about peering down into a well, the blind seer glimpses the heavens at the bottom, while the poet/listener, Heaney suggests, is "cured" by learning to see like Rosie Keenan, that is, *through* the earthly to the empyrean beyond.

The last poem in *The Spirit Level*, is a beautiful sixteen-liner titled "Postscript."

Here, the speaker records an epiphanal moment that occurred while driving along the coast of County Clare, when brilliant light flashes off the ocean on one side, and on the other side the surface of a "slate-grey lake is lit / By the earthed lightning of a flock of swans" (1998, 411). All is action and movement—the ocean "wild" with "foam and glitter," the swans' feathers "roughed and ruffling," their heads "tucked or cresting or busy underwater." Struck by the rapturous beauty and energy of the scene, the speaker also recognizes its fleetingness and that it is "Useless to think you'll park and capture it / More thoroughly." Speaker and reader are caught in a spatial and temporal metaxic "in between" moment, a lovely glimpsed ideal manifested here in the glimmering light and motion of the actual world. "You are neither here nor there," the speaker reminds us. We live in "a hurry through which known and strange things pass," yet where sudden flashes of revelation can "catch the heart off guard and blow it open."

On one level, "Postscript" is an invitation to the reader to focus his attention on such fleeting manifestations of "light" in the world. It is an invitation to follow the speaker's path:

> And some time make the time to drive out west
> Into County Clare, along the Flaggy Shore
> In September or October.

It invites the reader not merely into journeying but also into a way of seeing the world. Thus, like the opening poem in the volume, "The Rain Stick," it is a poem about poetry and poetry's valuable relation to ordinary experience as a mode of vision. As an addended postscript, an afterword, it points to Thomas Hardy's "Afterwards," a poem Heaney discussed in the introduction to *The Redress of Poetry*. There, Heaney celebrated Hardy's lyric as a prime example of poetry's power to "transform the familiar into something rich and strange," to manifest its "world-renewing potential," and to bring "human existence into fuller life." Poetry contains that capacity, Heaney insists, because it exists on the frontier between the actual and the imagined ideal, exists in the metaxu, and because of this it is able, through language, to give consciousness "access to a dimension beyond the frontier"; i.e., access to the transcendent (1995, xvi–xvii).

One of the ways in which "Postscript" transforms the familiar into something rich and strange and opens access to the transcendent is by the brilliantly paradoxical counterbalancing of its argument and its achieved form. Caught in the fleeting moments of a beautiful epiphany of nature's wonders, the speaker says, sadly but realistically: "Useless to think you'll park and capture it / More thoroughly." But in fact the poem itself reverses that statement, because it fully captures the fleeting moment by the power, energy, and movement of its language. Stated differently, in the midst of life's fleeting events "Postscript" creates that hieratic "riff in time" that brings us to full awareness of our own transitory, yet transcendently unique and valuable, presence in the world.

In "The Love of God and Affliction," Weil said: "The beauty of the world gives us an intimation of its claim to a place in our heart. In the beauty of the world brute necessity becomes an object of love. What is more beautiful than the action of gravity on the fugitive folds of the sea waves, or the almost eternal folds of the mountains?" (1951, 128–29) In "Postscript," the beauty of the world, of the grace of "light" within the metaxu, works to "catch the heart off guard and blow it open." Such beauty makes the world an "object of love" that true poetry can manifest, and as Heaney said, insofar as it does this it manifests poetry's redemptive capacities because it affirms to the fullest the heights and depths of our spiritual being.

POSTSCRIPT

At the conclusion of *The Witness of Poetry*, in a lecture titled "On Hope," Czeslaw Milosz observed that the current culture suffers from "a reductionist Weltanschuung professed universally today" (1983, 109). Stated differently, that reductionist worldview can be described as submission to the force of gravity absent any acknowledgement of the metaphysical dimension of reality. Despite this situation, Milosz expressed the hope that this reductionist worldview "will be superceded by another vision better adapted to the complexity of the world and of individuals" (109). Milosz placed his hope in the emergence of a new historical consciousness, one that would explore "the exceptionality, strangeness, and loneliness of that creature mysterious to itself, a being necessarily transcending its own limits" (110). This new historical consciousness would include awareness of the metaphysical dimension of reality, for as Milosz argued elsewhere, man is a metaphysical being who cannot simply be reduced to history (2001, 215). Moreover, he believed this new consciousness would focus its attention not on the future but on the past, "contemplating its entire past, searching for a key to its own enigma, and penetrating, through empathy, the soul of bygone generations and of whole civilizations" (1983, 110).

Simone Weil held out a similar hope. Thinking of the same reductionist worldview Milosz described, she posed the central question: "From where will a renewal come to us, to us who have spoiled and devastated the whole earthly globe?" Her answer, as Milosz reports, is simply: "Only from the past, if we love it" (114). For Weil, love of the past is the key to renewal and self-transcendence because it manifests "two things [which] cannot be reduced to any rationalism: Time and Beauty." The distance of time purifies reality, and "reality seen that way is beautiful. . . . Distance is the soul of beauty" (114). Reflecting upon Weil's hope for renewal, Milosz reminds us that Dostoevsky, "skeptical as he was about the fate of civilization . . . affirmed that the world would be saved by beauty" (115).

Like Milosz and Weil, Heaney in his poetry affirms such a new historical consciousness. The poet's task is to develop and express what he called a "more inclusive" consciousness open to the metaphysical dimension of reality, to the transcendent, and to grace. It is to redress the imbalance of the reductionist worldview and liberate the human spirit by performing what Yeats called "the spiritual intellect's great work." Insofar as his poems accomplish this feat, they express hope by transforming the past into beautiful works of art as Yeats did in "Lapis Lazuli"—"gaiety transfiguring all that dread." But Heaney is also well aware that a retrogression from inclusive consciousness and full human-ity is also possible, as poems like "Sibyl," "Punishment," and "Weighing In" clearly demonstrate. The choice of "saurian relapses" into violence, stupidity, and close-mindedness by those Heaney refers to as "anvil brains" is always near at hand. Simone Weil saw the same retrogression throughout history—Homer's Troy as prelude to Caesar's Rome and Hitler's Germany.

For Weil the philosopher, the spiritual counterbalance to the gravity of a reductionist worldview is to be found explicitly in the crucified Jesus. The Cross, for her, is the paradoxical *axis mundi* of human suffering and divine love that "transfigures all that dread" and verifies our full humanity because it rests ultimately on God's mysterious love. Heaney is a poet, not a philosopher or mystic. As a poet, he is more self-consciously embedded in the historical flux, more questioning of traditional Christian assumptions, and never at ease with the consolations of philosophy or religious belief. For Heaney the poet, the spiritual counterbalance to the gravity of a reductionist worldview is rooted in the quotidian world and in the imagination's power to disclose spirit in matter. Thus his poetry is incarnational in the truest sense. As he says, "praise the verity of gravel" and "walk on air against your better judge-ment." Spirit is elusive and manifests itself obliquely in his poems, but it is the informing *gestalt* and numen behind his love of nature, of friendship, of communal bonds, and of his hopes for the future. I believe that ultimately, like Weil, the core of his vision is a power of love that can "catch the heart off guard and blow it open," that can be seen in stray sprigs of mint in a field, in the light of a single dewdrop, or in the "breath of life / In a breath of air, a lime-green butterfly / Crossing the pilgrims' sun-struck *via crusis*."

As Daniel Tobin's admirable study has shown, Heaney's best poems take us to the borders of transcendent vision, a vantage point of light that intimates, but only intimates, a greater reality beyond. The light itself suggests a gravity-defying force of ultimate meaning and of love, in the universe, a real force whose mystery is just beyond the power of human vision and human expression. At the end of the *Paradiso*, the poet-pilgrim Dante achieved the full beatific vision. In "A Dream of Solstice," Heaney's adaptation of Dante's epiphanic experience, he offers a measured response to the possibilities of such a vision in our time by measuring our hard realities against the hope-filled coming of light. In the poem, the speaker watches a sunrise as the light enters the megalithic tomb at Newgrange on a cold December morning:

> the milted glow
> Of sunrise, for an eastern dazzle
> To send first light like share-shine in a furrow
>
> Steadily deeper, farther available,
> Creeping along the floor of the passage grave
> To backstone and capstone, to hold its candle
>
> Inside the cosmic hill. Who dares say "love"
> At this cold coming? Who would not dare say it?
> Is this the moved wheel that the poet spoke of,
>
> The star-pivot? Life's perseid in the ashpit
> Of the dead? Like his, my speech cannot
> Tell what the mind needs told: an infant tongue
>
> Milky with breast milk would be more articulate. (1999)

It is difficult to say—or not say—"love" at this "cold coming." Such is the truth of our times. The absolute certitude of Dante the pilgrim is unavailable, though the poet can still affirm its possibility. The challenge, as Weil said, is "to love God through and across the destruction of Troy and Carthage—and with no consolation. Love is not consolation, it is light" (1997, 59).

3. Daniel Tobin does not point out that Adorno later retracted his statement and said that the Holocaust was a fit subject for poetry.
4. J. C. Bloem, n.d., *After Liberation*, trans. Cliff Crego. http://c-smusic.com/features/r2c-index.html.
5. Micha F. Lindemans, "Chukwu," *Encyclopedia Mythica*, 1995–2006. http://www.pantheon.org/articles/c/chukwu.html.

NOTES

1. Many critics, including Eugene O'Brien, Michael, Parker, Daniel Tob[...] Neil Corcoran have discussed Jung's influence on Heaney. The poet noted this influence in his essay "Place and Displacement: Recent Poe[...] Northern Ireland" (2002, 122–46).
2. Voegelin's concept of the deformation of being in modernity is develop[...] sively throughout his multivolume *Order and History* and particula[...] *Anamnesis* and in *Science, Politics and Gnosticism*. For a convenient o[...] his thought, see Niemeyer 1976.
3. Percy, "Notes for a Novel about the End of the World" (1975, 113).
4. Weil, "The Love of God and Affliction" (1951, 128).
5. Weil, "The *Iliad*: Poem of Might" (Panichas 1977, 153–84).
6. Eric O. Springsted, "Contradiction, Mystery, and the Use of Word[...] and Springsted 1966, 23).
7. Thomas Werge, "Sacramental Tension: Divine Transcendence and [...] in Simone Weil's Literary Imagination" (Dunaway and Springsted [...]
8. J. Huby, *Mystiques paulinienne et johanique* (Durrwell 1960, 54).
9. George Herbert, "The Pulley" (Heaney 1955, 11–12).
10. It is interesting to note that W. B. Yeats, in reference to Wilfred [...] that passive suffering was not a fit subject for poetry. Heaney re[...] ment in his poem in memory of Ted Hughes, "On His Worl[...] Tongue": "Passive suffering: who said it was disallowed / As a t[...] Already in *Beowulf* / The dumb-founding of woe, the stunt an[...] in-hiding is the best of it." See also Heaney 1989a, 64.
11. See Simone Weil's comments on work (1977, 232–36).
12. In the light of these formal and thematic complexities, Helen [...] tation of the poem as an example of Heaney's essential stoic[...] plistic to account adequately for the poem's nuances (Vendl[...]

WORKS CITED

Andrews, Elmer, ed. 1998. *The Poetry of Seamus Heaney*. New York: Columbia University Press.

Baker, J M., Jr. 2005. "Nostalgia of Everyday: Earthly Things as Poetic Criteria in Weil and Jacottet." *Christianity and Literature* 55, no. 1, 73–93.

Barfield, Owen. 1965. *Saving the Appearances: A Study in Idolatry*. New York: Harcourt, Brace and World.

Bloem, J. C. "After Liberation." In *Straight Roads, Slow Rivers, Deep Clay: New Translations of Contemporary Dutch Poetry*. Trans. Cliff Crago. http://www.cs-music.com/features/snowdoor.html#Bevrijding.

Brueck, Katherine T. 1995. *The Redemption of Tragedy: The Literary Vision of Simone Weil*. Albany: State University of New York Press.

Buber, Martin. 1952. *Eclipse of God*. New York: Harper.

Collins, Floyd. 2003. *Seamus Heaney: The Crisis of Identity*. Newark: University of Delaware Press.

Dargan, Joan. 1999. *Simone Weil: Thinking Poetically*. Albany: State University of New York Press.

Dunaway, John M., and Eric O. Springsted, eds. 1996. *The Beauty That Saves: Essays on Aesthetics and Language in Simone Weil*. Macon, GA: Mercer University Press.

Durrwell, F. X. 1960. *The Resurrection*. Trans. Rosemary Sheed. New York: Sheed and Ward.

Ellis, John M. 1989. *Against Deconstruction*. Princeton, NJ: Princeton University Press.

Fiori, Gabriella. 1989. *Simone Weil: An Intellectual Biography*. Trans. Joseph R. Berrigan. Athens: University of Georgia Press.

Fitzgerald, Robert, trans. 1998. *The Odyssey*, by Homer. New York: Ferrar, Straus and Giroux.

Frost, Robert. 1963. *Selected Poems of Robert Frost*. New York: Holt, Rinehart and Winston.

Hart, Henry. 1992. *Seamus Heaney: Poet of Contrary Progressions*. Syracuse, NY: Syracuse University Press.

Heaney, Seamus. 1966. *Death of a Naturalist*. London: Faber and Faber.

———. 1972. *Wintering Out*. New York: Oxford University Press.

———. 1980a. *Preoccupations: Selected Prose, 1968–1978*. New York: Farrar, Straus and Giroux.

———. 1980b. *Selected Poems, 1965–1975*. London: Faber and Faber.

———. 1987. *The Haw Lantern*. London: Faber and Faber.

———. 1989a. *The Government of the Tongue: Selected Prose, 1978–1987*. New York: Farrar, Straus and Giroux.

———. 1989b. *The Place of Writing*. Atlanta, GA: Scholars Press.

———. 1990. *Selected Poems, 1966–1987*. New York: Farrar, Straus and Giroux.

———. 1991. *Seeing Things*. London: Faber and Faber.

———. 1995. *The Redress of Poetry*. New York: Farrar, Straus and Giroux.

———. 1996. *The Spirit Level*. New York: Farrar, Straus and Giroux.

———. 1998. *Opened Ground: Selected Poems, 1966–1996*. New York: Farrar, Straus and Giroux.

———. 1999. "A Dream of Solstice." *Irish Times*. December 21. http://www.ireland.com/newspaper/frontpage/1999/1221/99122100002.html.

———. 2000. *Beowulf*. New York: Farrar, Straus and Giroux.

———. 2001. *Electric Light*. New York: Farrar, Straus and Giroux.

———. 2002. *Finders, Keepers: Selected Prose, 1971–2001*. New York: Farrar, Straus and Giroux.

Hermida, J. Ranilo B. 2006. "Simone Weil: A Sense of God." *Logos* 9, no. 1, 127–44.

Jung, Carl G. ca. 1950. *Modern Man in Search of a Soul*. Trans. W. S. Dell and Cary F. Baynes. New York: Harcourt.

Lindemans, Micha F. "Chukwu." In *Encyclopedia Mythica*. http://www.pantheon.org/articles/c/chukwu.html.

Lynch, William F. 1960. *Christ and Apollo: The Dimensions of the Literary Imagination*. New York: Sheed.

Miller, Karl. 2000. *Seamus Heaney in Conversation with Karl Miller*. London: Between the Lines.

Milosz, Czeslaw. 1983. *The Witness of Poetry*. Cambridge, MA: Harvard University Press.

———. 2001. *To Begin Where I Am: Selected Essays*. Ed. Bogdana Carpenter and Madeline J. Levine. New York: Farrar, Straus and Giroux.

Nevin, Thomas R. 1991. *Simone Weil: Portrait of a Self-Exiled Jew*. Chapel Hill: University of North Carolina Press.

Niemeyer, Gerhardt. 1976. "Eric Voegelin and the Drama of Mankind." *Modern Age* 20: 35.

O'Brien, Eugene. 2003. *Seamus Heaney: Searches for Answers*. London: Pluto.

O'Connor, Flannery. 1969. *Mystery and Manners: Occasional Prose*. Ed. Sally and Robert Fitzgerald. New York: Farrar, Straus and Giroux.

O'Donoghue, Bernard. 1994. *Seamus Heaney and the Language of Poetry*. New York: Harvester: Wheatsheaf.

Panichas, George A., ed. 1977. *The Simone Weil Reader*. Wakefield, RI: Moyer Bell.

Parker, Michael. 1993. *Seamus Heaney: The Making of a Poet*. Iowa City: University of Iowa Press.

Percy, Walker. 1975. *The Message in the Bottle: How Queer Man Is, How Queer Language Is, and What One Has to Do with the Other*. New York: Farrar, Straus and Giroux.

Pétrement, Simone. 1976. *Simone Weil: A Life*. Trans. Raymond Rosenthal. New York: Pantheon.

Springsted, Eric O. 1983. *Christus Mediator: Platonic Mediation in the Thought of Simone Weil*. Chico, CA: Scholars Press.

Steiner, George. 2001. *Grammars of Creation*. New Haven, CT: Yale University Press.

Tobin, Daniel. 1999. *Passage to the Center: Imagination and the Sacred in the Poetry of Seamus Heaney*. Lexington: University of Kentucky Press.

Vendler, Helen. 1998. *Seamus Heaney*. Cambridge, MA: Harvard University Press.

Voegelin, Eric. 2000. *Collected Works*. Vol. 10. Ed. Ellis Santos. Baton Rouge: Louisiana State University Press.

Weil, Simone. 1951. *Waiting for Gxod*. Tran. Emma Craufurd. Introduction by Leslie Fiedler. New York: Harper and Row.

———. 1970. *First and Last Notebooks*. Trans. Richard Rees. London: Oxford University Press.

————. 1997. *Gravity and Grace*. Trans. Arthur Wills. Introductions by Gustave Thibon and Thomas R. Nevin. Lincoln: University of Nebraska Press.

Whitehead, Alfred North. 1925. *Science and the Modern World*. New York: MacMillan.

INDEX

13. Daniel Tobin does not point out that Adorno later retracted his statement and said that the Holocaust was a fit subject for poetry.
14. J. C. Bloem, n.d., *After Liberation*, trans. Cliff Crego. http://c-smusic.com/features/r2c-index.html.
15. Micha F. Lindemans, "Chukwu," *Encyclopedia Mythica*, 1995–2006. http://www.pantheon.org/articles/c/chukwu.html.

NOTES

1. Many critics, including Eugene O'Brien, Michael, Parker, Daniel Tobin, and Neil Corcoran have discussed Jung's influence on Heaney. The poet himself noted this influence in his essay "Place and Displacement: Recent Poetry from Northern Ireland" (2002, 122–46).

2. Voegelin's concept of the deformation of being in modernity is developed extensively throughout his multivolume *Order and History* and particularly in his *Anamnesis* and in *Science, Politics and Gnosticism*. For a convenient overview of his thought, see Niemeyer 1976.

3. Percy, "Notes for a Novel about the End of the World" (1975, 113).

4. Weil, "The Love of God and Affliction" (1951, 128).

5. Weil, "The *Iliad*: Poem of Might" (Panichas 1977, 153–84).

6. Eric O. Springsted, "Contradiction, Mystery, and the Use of Words" (Dunaway and Springsted 1966, 23).

7. Thomas Werge, "Sacramental Tension: Divine Transcendence and Finite Images in Simone Weil's Literary Imagination" (Dunaway and Springsted 1966, 85–99).

8. J. Huby, *Mystiques paulinienne et johanique* (Durrwell 1960, 54).

9. George Herbert, "The Pulley" (Heaney 1955, 11–12).

10. It is interesting to note that W. B. Yeats, in reference to Wilfred Owen, argued that passive suffering was not a fit subject for poetry. Heaney rejected this argument in his poem in memory of Ted Hughes, "On His Work in the English Tongue": "Passive suffering: who said it was disallowed / As a theme for poetry? Already in *Beowulf* / The dumb-founding of woe, the stunt and stress / of hurt-in-hiding is the best of it." See also Heaney 1989a, 64.

11. See Simone Weil's comments on work (1977, 232–36).

12. In the light of these formal and thematic complexities, Helen Vendler's interpretation of the poem as an example of Heaney's essential stoicism seems too simplistic to account adequately for the poem's nuances (Vendler 1998, 159–64).

WORKS CITED

Andrews, Elmer, ed. 1998. *The Poetry of Seamus Heaney*. New York: Columbia University Press.

Baker, J. M., Jr. 2005. "Nostalgia of Everyday: Earthly Things as Poetic Criteria in Weil and Jacottet." *Christianity and Literature* 55, no. 1, 73–93.

Barfield, Owen. 1965. *Saving the Appearances: A Study in Idolatry*. New York: Harcourt, Brace and World.

Bloem, J. C. "After Liberation." In *Straight Roads, Slow Rivers, Deep Clay: New Translations of Contemporary Dutch Poetry*. Trans. Cliff Crago. http://www.cs-music.com/features/snowdoor.html#Bevrijding.

Brueck, Katherine T. 1995. *The Redemption of Tragedy: The Literary Vision of Simone Weil*. Albany: State University of New York Press.

Buber, Martin. 1952. *Eclipse of God*. New York: Harper.

Collins, Floyd. 2003. *Seamus Heaney: The Crisis of Identity*. Newark: University of Delaware Press.

Dargan, Joan. 1999. *Simone Weil: Thinking Poetically*. Albany: State University of New York Press.

Dunaway, John M., and Eric O. Springsted, eds. 1996. *The Beauty That Saves: Essays on Aesthetics and Language in Simone Weil*. Macon, GA: Mercer University Press.

Durrwell, F. X. 1960. *The Resurrection*. Trans. Rosemary Sheed. New York: Sheed and Ward.

Ellis, John M. 1989. *Against Deconstruction*. Princeton, NJ: Princeton University Press.

Fiori, Gabriella. 1989. *Simone Weil: An Intellectual Biography*. Trans. Joseph R. Berrigan. Athens: University of Georgia Press.

Fitzgerald, Robert, trans. 1998. *The Odyssey*, by Homer. New York: Ferrar, Straus and Giroux.

Frost, Robert. 1963. *Selected Poems of Robert Frost*. New York: Holt, Rinehart and Winston.

Hart, Henry. 1992. *Seamus Heaney: Poet of Contrary Progressions*. Syracuse, NY: Syracuse University Press.

Heaney, Seamus. 1966. *Death of a Naturalist*. London: Faber and Faber.

———. 1972. *Wintering Out*. New York: Oxford University Press.

———. 1980a. *Preoccupations: Selected Prose, 1968–1978*. New York: Farrar, Straus and Giroux.

———. 1980b. *Selected Poems, 1965–1975*. London: Faber and Faber.

———. 1987. *The Haw Lantern*. London: Faber and Faber.

———. 1989a. *The Government of the Tongue: Selected Prose, 1978–1987*. New York: Farrar, Straus and Giroux.

———. 1989b. *The Place of Writing*. Atlanta, GA: Scholars Press.

———. 1990. *Selected Poems, 1966–1987*. New York: Farrar, Straus and Giroux.

———. 1991. *Seeing Things*. London: Faber and Faber.

———. 1995. *The Redress of Poetry*. New York: Farrar, Straus and Giroux.

———. 1996. *The Spirit Level*. New York: Farrar, Straus and Giroux.

———. 1998. *Opened Ground: Selected Poems, 1966–1996*. New York: Farrar, Straus and Giroux.

———. 1999. "A Dream of Solstice." *Irish Times*. December 21. http://www.ireland.com/newspaper/frontpage/1999/1221/99122100002.html.

———. 2000. *Beowulf*. New York: Farrar, Straus and Giroux.

———. 2001. *Electric Light*. New York: Farrar, Straus and Giroux.

———. 2002. *Finders, Keepers: Selected Prose, 1971–2001*. New York: Farrar, Straus and Giroux.

Hermida, J. Ranilo B. 2006. "Simone Weil: A Sense of God." *Logos* 9, no. 1, 127–44.

Jung, Carl G. ca. 1950. *Modern Man in Search of a Soul*. Trans. W. S. Dell and Cary F. Baynes. New York: Harcourt.

Lindemans, Micha F. "Chukwu." In *Encyclopedia Mythica*. http://www.pantheon.org/articles/c/chukwu.html.

Lynch, William F. 1960. *Christ and Apollo: The Dimensions of the Literary Imagination*. New York: Sheed.

Miller, Karl. 2000. *Seamus Heaney in Conversation with Karl Miller*. London: Between the Lines.

Milosz, Czeslaw. 1983. *The Witness of Poetry*. Cambridge, MA: Harvard University Press.

———. 2001. *To Begin Where I Am: Selected Essays*. Ed. Bogdana Carpenter and Madeline J. Levine. New York: Farrar, Straus and Giroux.

Nevin, Thomas R. 1991. *Simone Weil: Portrait of a Self-Exiled Jew*. Chapel Hill: University of North Carolina Press.

Niemeyer, Gerhardt. 1976. "Eric Voegelin and the Drama of Mankind." *Modern Age* 20: 35.

O'Brien, Eugene. 2003. *Seamus Heaney: Searches for Answers*. London: Pluto.

O'Connor, Flannery. 1969. *Mystery and Manners: Occasional Prose*. Ed. Sally and Robert Fitzgerald. New York: Farrar, Straus and Giroux.

O'Donoghue, Bernard. 1994. *Seamus Heaney and the Language of Poetry*. New York: Harvester: Wheatsheaf.

Panichas, George A., ed. 1977. *The Simone Weil Reader*. Wakefield, RI: Moyer Bell.

Parker, Michael. 1993. *Seamus Heaney: The Making of a Poet*. Iowa City: University of Iowa Press.

Percy, Walker. 1975. *The Message in the Bottle: How Queer Man Is, How Queer Language Is, and What One Has to Do with the Other*. New York: Farrar, Straus and Giroux.

Pétrement, Simone. 1976. *Simone Weil: A Life*. Trans. Raymond Rosenthal. New York: Pantheon.

Springsted, Eric O. 1983. *Christus Mediator: Platonic Mediation in the Thought of Simone Weil*. Chico, CA: Scholars Press.

Steiner, George. 2001. *Grammars of Creation*. New Haven, CT: Yale University Press.

Tobin, Daniel. 1999. *Passage to the Center: Imagination and the Sacred in the Poetry of Seamus Heaney*. Lexington: University of Kentucky Press.

Vendler, Helen. 1998. *Seamus Heaney*. Cambridge, MA: Harvard University Press.

Voegelin, Eric. 2000. *Collected Works*. Vol. 10. Ed. Ellis Santos. Baton Rouge: Louisiana State University Press.

Weil, Simone. 1951. *Waiting for Gxod*. Tran. Emma Craufurd. Introduction by Leslie Fiedler. New York: Harper and Row.

———. 1970. *First and Last Notebooks*. Trans. Richard Rees. London: Oxford University Press.

————. 1997. *Gravity and Grace*. Trans. Arthur Wills. Introductions by Gustave Thibon and Thomas R. Nevin. Lincoln: University of Nebraska Press.

Whitehead, Alfred North. 1925. *Science and the Modern World*. New York: MacMillan.

INDEX